The Happy Elementary School Teacher

*Self Care Habits to Avoid Burnout, De-Stress
And Take Care of Yourself*

Matilda Walsh

Table of Contents

Introduction

Congratulations, you're an elementary school teacher! You've got one of the most important and fulfilling careers in the world. But in order to avoid stress and burnout as a teacher, it's very important that you also take care of yourself.

Educators worldwide are expected to carefully educate the next generation by teaching them the skills and knowledge they will need to be successful in their lives. This role often results in teachers becoming a vital part of the lives of their students and often become someone they look up to. And many times, elementary school teachers can play a pivotal role in the lives of the boys and girls they teach .

We all know that teaching also comes with many challenges. This includes implementing the school's policies and procedures and working through the curriculum, while also dealing with discipline issues, stress and challenging situations. No two days in the classroom are the same.

Teachers tend to put their students' education and well-being above all else, so it can be hard to switch off teacher mode when you step outside the classroom. Feeling stressed in school, and not prioritizing your health and well-being as an elementary school teacher can lead to burnout. And burnout will affect all areas of your life - in the classroom and at home with your family.

Getting into a habit of not putting ourselves first and not allowing ourselves the time to take care of ourselves physically and mentally can really impact our bodies. From feeling tired to lower self-esteem, anxiety, and even depression. Taking care of your general well-being as a teacher is something that is easy and quite common to overlook when you are a busy educator.

Getting a good night's sleep, drinking water and eating nutritious food, feeling good about yourself, and creating healthy habits and goals are all steps to better your life. But not only this, these simple steps can make you a better educator and, in turn, a better role model for your students.

So if you're an elementary school teacher who is burnt out and stressed and needs to be reminded how to love yourself, organize, make time for yourself, and take care of your body and mind, I have good news. This book is for you!

When you are older, and you look back on the life you have lived and the students you have helped, what kind of life would you want to look back on? 40 years of being a stressed and tired teacher who lost their spark a few years in? Or someone who adored every moment they spent in the classroom, and who stayed fit & healthy, spent time with friends and family and had a fulfilling life outside of school too?

Your life has endless possibilities. It's time to prioritize setting accomplishable goals, checking in with yourself, trying some new habits that will have a positive change to your daily life and most importantly, pulling yourself out of the rut many of us find ourselves in.

It is not an overnight job; sometimes, it might be challenging to take the steps you need to achieve the lifestyle you want as an elementary school teacher.

But these changes won't just affect you, though this is what it is predominantly about. You'll also lead by example and show your students the importance of taking care of themselves, staying healthy and creating a healthy work-life balance. You can even use some ideas from this book in your class - to promote similar goals for your students!

So it's time to ask yourself the ultimate question: Are you 100% happy with every aspect of your current life? With your health? With your happiness and stress levels? And if the answer is anything but a resounding unquestioning yes, then maybe it's time to find some small but powerful ways to start getting your life on the path you want it to be.

Handy tip: Implement the tips and strategies in this book with a friend! Form a small book club with your colleagues and read one chapter each week.

Chapter 1: Sleep

We have all been in a situation where we walk into our classrooms and see tired faces looking back at us. Those tired faces mean insufficient sleep, bad tempers, and a lack of concentration. The effects of your student's lack of sleep should prove one thing: lack of sleep will affect everyone in many ways, not just students. If you show up to school with little to no rest, you may feel unmotivated, unorganized, and underwhelming to your students. So if you want to improve your mood, make handling tricky situations in and out of school much easier and increase your energy in the classroom, it is time to fix your sleep habits!

There is compelling scientific evidence that sleep plays an important role in many biological functions critical to maintaining all body systems. Adults should typically aim for 7-9 hours of sleep per night.

Adults who do not get enough sleep are more likely to suffer from cardiovascular issues, immune system deterioration, increased risk of obesity and type II diabetes, and cognitive and memory impairment. This is not good! Not only can sleep deprivation directly impact your brain, but it can also affect your mood and behavior and be linked directly to mental health struggles, including anxiety and depression. These mental health struggles can directly impact your teaching ability if left untreated.

The benefits of sleep for cognitive functions like memory and insight formations - the foundations of learning, creativity, and scientific discovery - are also lost due to sleep deprivation. If you feel tired and run down, how are you supposed to deliver your lessons in an engaging way that will delight your students?

Understanding the quality of your sleep and how it impacts your life is essential. We can all wake up feeling restless sometimes, and this can affect our entire day's work - and lack of energy in the evenings too. Reviewing and adjusting your habits around your sleep schedule can dramatically improve your overall quality of sleep and therefore allow your body to heal and rest to prepare for each day.

The Basics of Sleep

Teaching isn't a career that ends when the school bell rings. Often we bring work home or we might need to plan things out at home for the coming days. This strain on our work-life balance can lead to late nights hunched over a desk, mapping out exercises and marking quizzes, and not allowing your body to wind down before you go to sleep.

As a society, there has been a major negative shift in not prioritizing your sleep over other commitments in your life. Being busy all the time - and working all hours of the day and some of the night - is seen by some as a badge of honor!

We are sleeping less, going to bed later and getting up earlier - especially if we have kids or a long commute - to the point where for some feeling tired from a lack of sleep has become totally normal every day.

Meanwhile, road collisions are rising, with 33% of deaths on the road being attributed to fatigue and many end-of-life conditions having evidence relating to sleep deprivation. With statistics such as these, we must start addressing our sleep concerns and figuring out why we aren't getting the correct amounts to function properly.

There are varying theories relating to the reasoning behind why we sleep and the processes the body undertakes while sleeping. Sigmund Freud stated the need for sleep to form dreams essential to reducing psychic pressure and minimizing the potential for psychotic episodes, which hints at the psychological benefits of sleeping. So using this analysis, it is understandable how your mood can be directly impacted by behavioral implications, especially when sleep-deprived and dealing with children.

Ivan Pavlov and Nathaniel Kleitman are credited with being the pioneers of the concept that we are conditioned by the setting sun and other sleep triggers. This theory is commonly accepted and links to the ideals of having a body clock that naturally wakes you based on exposure to daylight, with physiological changes evident in this stage, including the activation of hormone production relating to typical functions we have when awake.

Though there continue to be theories about why we sleep, some conclusions have been drawn from scientific studies that lean toward energy conservation and restoration theories. According to these hypotheses, our bodies undergo increased periods of muscle growth, tissue repair, and protein synthesis while asleep. We are allowing our bodies to recharge and reset during our sleeping periods. Various sleep cycle stages go as fast as a flash in our minds.

The average person has a basic understanding of sleep's many complexities. Every night, our bodies go through a series of sleep cycles that last anywhere from 90 to 110 minutes each and consist of five stages: stage one, stage two, stage three, stage four, and rapid eye movement (REM). An electroencephalogram, also known as an EEG, is a device that measures the electrical activity in the brain. Scientists use this device to measure brain waves and see the different stages. The first stage we enter, known as stage 1, is typically characterized by a very light sleep from which one can easily rouse. During this stage, some people have reported experiencing hypnic myoclonia, which is described as a sensation similar to falling.

After that, we move on to stage 2, where our brain waves become noticeably more sluggish, and our eyes become completely still.

After stage 2, our body moves into a deep sleep. When we reach stage 3, the activity in our brain has slowed down to delta waves, the slowest type of waves, with intermittent bursts of faster waves. Stage 4 is characterized by the presence of only delta waves, and there is no activity in the muscles; individuals who are asleep during this stage are notoriously challenging to awaken. After that, we transition into REM, also known as the rapid eye movement stage of sleep.

During rapid eye movement (REM), our eyes move quickly, our heart rate increases, and we experience atonia, the paralysis of our muscles. We also dream during this stage. We spend significantly less time in deep sleep as the cycles continue throughout the night. As a result, by the time the sun begins to rise and morning arrives, we have generally only been sleeping in stages 1, 2, and REM (Ryan, 2016).

We accumulate a sleep debt while we are awake, which is "paid off" while we sleep. Although individuals differ, you need roughly one hour of sleep for every two hours awake. This debt builds up over several nights when we don't get the required rest. According to research, the brain can "remember" this debt for a few weeks. Astonishingly, the accumulated sleep debt can significantly impact mental and motor skills, and William Dement has extensively documented this.

The performance levels of volunteers who were only allowed four hours of sleep per night for two weeks were equivalent to those of subjects who were kept awake nonstop for three days and nights. One late night could have ramifications that last the rest of the week. So what is it you are prioritizing over your precious sleep?

Night Habits

Setting up healthy habits before bed can hugely increase your sleep quality. Eating late at night while scrolling social media on your phone is probably going to hinder your ability to fall asleep! As a teacher, you might enjoy the comfort of a warm cup of coffee in the staffroom on your lunch break or after school. However, recent research has shown negative evidence of the impact of what some might see as a harmless cup of coffee on your much-needed rest.

Coffee

Firstly, minimizing your caffeine consumption with enough time to let your body process it before sleep, not only aids digestion but also allows your body to focus on the mechanisms that take place during sleep.

Because caffeinated energy drinks are becoming increasingly popular and premium coffee contains a high amount of caffeine, it is safe to assume if you are regularly consuming caffeinated beverages after school hours, it may directly impact your rest. Increased caffeine consumption in younger age groups, which coincides with an increase in the prevalence of chronic sleep restriction. Recent research has shown that among samples, 37% of people reported using caffeine for the first time that day at 5 p.m. or later. The study suggested that caffeine consumed 6 hours before bedtime significantly disrupts sleep. This finding provides sleep recommendations that recommend avoiding substantial caffeine consumption for a minimum of 6 hours before you intend to go to sleep (Drake et al., 2013).

Bed

Understanding the conditions that suit you when you sleep and how your bedroom environment might jeopardize a good night's sleep is essential. Having comfortable bedding is crucial, with many people having differing preferences from a hard to a soft pillow-topped mattress. The important thing is finding what is comfortable for you, and a good mattress is worth the investment as you spend a large portion of your time in bed sleeping.

The same goes for the comfortability of bedding, and if your pillows are old and flat and provide no support to your head and neck, you will likely be readjusting throughout the night, limiting your sleep quality. The surface you sleep on is a crucial and often overlooked step to ensuring your sleep is comfortable. However, regardless of the quality of your bedding, many other factors relating to environmental interruptions can be made within your bedroom that can directly impact your sleep.

Light, noise and distractions

If you are on a busy street, try using blackout blinds or curtains to avoid any light entering the space while you are asleep. Try to test different options that can aid in sleep, including white noise. Many free apps can play a wide array of sounds to aid sleep from rainforest sounds, rain, or light humming. Though some people prefer a fan running when they sleep, supplying not only the white noise needed but also temperature control. Some people prefer sleeping with the television, but many studies suggest turning off technologies to avoid eye strain or racing thoughts before sleeping.

This goes along with taking time away from your phone and social media. Excessive social media before bed is directly connected to sleeping difficulties. That's why turning off your notifications and setting down your phone can have good results on your quality of sleep.

Night-time routine

Establish a nighttime routine that indicates to your mind and body that you intend to sleep. A simple self-care regime that makes you feel good and relaxes you is always worthwhile to implement at night time. This self-care routine could include essential grooming and bathing, skincare, and brushing teeth. Of course, you can add as many or as few steps to this routine, although making these steps into a positive ritual can lead to a healthy sleep habit.

Meditation and journaling

Washing your face and teeth is pretty standard practice, but what about ways to calm your mind and put the stresses of being an educator to the side for the night? Bringing yourself to the point of self-reflection before bed lets you relax your mind and allow yourself time to rest.

Self-reflection can be through the means of meditation, journaling, or giving gratitude. It doesn't have to be comprehensive but enough to provide yourself with the time alone with your mind and reflect on the day.

Although these steps seem simple, slight adjustments can help maintain a positive relationship with, prepare your body for, and support your overall ability to sleep. If there still seems to be trouble getting your 7-9 hours of sleep, or you're not even sure if your body knows how to get that sort of sleep, maybe it's worth considering tracking your sleep and seeing if you're allowing yourself the time you need.

Tracking your Sleep

Allowing yourself the time to sleep is essential. It can be very useful indeed to start tracking when you are sleeping. Using a journal to see how many hours you sleep is an option, though some nights might be easier to get to sleep than others, in which case the journal may not depict precisely how many hours you slept versus staring up at your bedroom ceiling.

To avoid starting the attraction of just one more episode on Netflix or whatever holds your attention before bed, having a set time to get into bed will definitely help. This could be done by setting the alarm on your phone and giving yourself the heads up that you have half an hour until it's time to get to bed.

Setting the alarm to go to bed might seem odd, but it is an excellent start to understanding how much time you give yourself to sleep. Everyone loves a good sleep-in on a weekend morning. This can still be accomplished by adjusting these set alarms to allow yourself the right amount of sleep without going over the recommended amount. Some say that if you notice you are not getting the correct amount of sleep, adjusting the alarm wake up time to ensure you wake up at the end of the sleep cycle can help you feel more refreshed - regardless of the hours of sleep, though you should try your best to aim for the 7-9 hours.

Sleep technology

There are many different types of sleep trackers. There are portable devices that can be placed on your bed to the built-in phone apps that can listen to changes in breathing or snoring and also monitor your body movement through the night.

Several apps that claim to measure and track snoring are even available!

These apps can give you a good understanding of how many hours you sleep on average each night. For accurate measurements of sleep and disturbances, a medical sleep study might be a solution to address further sleep concerns, but utilizing these available apps is a good stepping stone for most people to understand the basics of getting a good night's sleep.

Medical intervention

Sometimes changing your habits around your sleep may not be enough to improve your sleep. Getting 8 hours of sleep but still waking up tired could indicate a bigger problem with your rest. Whether you struggle to stay awake, get to sleep, or stay asleep can be a sign of identifiable sleep disorders. These can be attributed to caffeine intake, negative thoughts, and anxiety. These also have varying treatments and need to be addressed by professionals to understand the root causes of these disorders further.

You would need to complete a medical sleep study that tracks brain waves and analyzes the various stages of sleep you cycle through throughout the night to get precise information about your sleeping patterns. These studies are helpful in the diagnosis of sleep disorders like sleep apnea and insomnia. Sleep disorders are common among US adults, with 50-70 million reporting a sleep disorder. Insomnia is the most common specific sleep disorder, with short-term issues reported by about 30% of adults and chronic insomnia affecting about 10%. On the other hand, obstructive sleep apnea affects sleep quality by identifying frequent breathing pauses throughout your sleep cycles, restricting oxygen to the brain, and waking you. Obstructive sleep apnea affects women and men differently, with 9-21% of women and 24-34% of men in the US (American Sleep Association, 2018).

Most sleep disorders need intervention by medical professionals, using the sleep disorders mentioned above of sleep apnea and insomnia as examples.

Take Action

There is an expectation for teachers to be high energy at all times, especially when teaching elementary school students. Maintaining energy throughout the day depends largely on the quality of sleep you receive throughout the night and optimizing the ability to get a good night's sleep. This chapter pointed out some options to improve your relationship with rest, independently, or with professional advice.

The first thing for you to do is identify things that may disrupt your sleep, whether it be your bedding, exposed light, sounds, or what you do before you head to bed for the night. Do you consume caffeine later in the day? You should avoid caffeine, whether from a coffee or an energy drink, for up to six hours before you intend to go to sleep. So typically, after school would be out of the question unless you want caffeine in your system when trying to sleep. You could try switching to decaf or hot tea to minimize the amount of caffeine in your system as you try to sleep.

Try to prepare yourself to sleep mentally, set a time to get to bed, and maybe even consider setting the alarm to notify you that you have X amount of time until you are expected to be in bed. Postpone stressful conversations about finances or plans until the following day, so you have the time to consider your options without taking away from your rest. Practicing gratitude can also allow your brain to relax and help you avoid racing thoughts while trying to sleep. What were you grateful for that happened today? Try to keep it positive.

Set up your environment to be a space for sleep. Invest in good quality bedding, and make your bed fresh and ready for you to jump in at night. If you like listening to white noise, find the sound that calms you, whether it be nature sounds or the sound of a fan running. Get the temperature right, make a nightly routine that calms your body and mind down, so you feel relaxed before you slide under the covers.

These steps will not change how you go about your general day; they might just completely alter your way of thinking for the coming day, including your overall health and mood. You will be more energized to take on the daily grind of being a teacher, entertaining and enthusiastic for your students. It's time to take your sleep seriously and see the changes it can make in your day to day life!

Actions steps I will complete:

Chapter 2: You are what you eat

Teachers are often preparing for their classes, helping other staff and sometimes helping their students well into their lunch break. Sometimes this can mean skipping your lunch during the workday, which can harm both your body and your energy levels.

Eating healthy is a standard part of maintaining a healthy lifestyle. Food in its simplest form is for energy, so depending on your energy output, such as exercise or being restricted in movement while you work, you may need to adjust your intake accordingly. Daily we are bombarded with information on social media about what we should eat to look a certain way. Diet culture has taken over all forms of media, constantly filling your minds with new trends to tackle trouble areas or break down our relationship with food. Foods are not inherently bad or good. Food is an energy source, and it is important to eat within your means to ensure that this excess isn't being stored as fat but being used as energy.

So with all this information being thrown at us, how do we know what to eat? Basing your meals around nutritious options leaves you feeling full, energized, and satisfied. Overeating regularly can tip the scale and make you unhealthy. In the coming chapter, we will address eating for a healthy heart through understanding your diet to include and minimize the eating of some foods; this is just one example of how eating can determine our overall health.

It is also crucial to involve a medical professional if your eating becomes problematic, whether it be skipping meals, forgetting to eat, labeling certain foods as 'bad,' or just not having a healthy relationship with food. The advice given in this book is not coming from a medical professional or nutritionist, so all advice should be taken with a grain of salt and should just be compared to the basic principle of eating healthier to better your day-to-day life.

Eating Habits

There is a multitude of evidence about eating behaviors consisting of habits. When a behavior is habitual, you will need little information to make decisions. These habits could include the idea of eating triggered by situational cues like sitting down to watch a movie. Your body connects this situation with snacking, like at a movie theater. Although not inheritably bad, using these autopilot mechanisms to improve your eating habits is better than encouraging late-night snacks or potential overeating. When discussing habitual eating, meal prepping could be beneficial in transferring these habits into healthier, productive ones while also giving a chance to try out new recipes, home cooking, and keeping track of your food intake.

Your eating routine

Sitting at a table can help you focus on the food you are eating, not with you staring at a television and not even looking at your plate as you eat.

Being present as you consume food will make you enjoy your food more and acknowledge every bite, often making you chew more and feel fuller quicker. Utilizing smaller plates can often trick the mind into thinking you have a larger serving. It may appear similar to being served on a large plate, which can mask just how large the portion may be.

Similarly, if you use small dishes for snacks, you are more likely to have a visual representation of the amount you are eating instead of eating directly out of a bag of chips or chocolate. Sometimes all it takes is simple visual cues to show your body what it is having. The body will also give cues when it has eaten enough. You do not need to feel overfed or bloated to know you are satisfied with a meal, nor do you need to finish what's on your plate just to finish what's on your plate. These shifts in understanding the food you consume and whether your body needs it are integral to having a healthy relationship with food. Focusing on what's going into your body will aid with understanding what your body needs, when it needs it and when it has had enough.

Eating away from your home environment can often be linked to eating more calorie-dense meals.

A night out with friends with a meal, a few sides, and a few beers or cocktails could equal almost double your daily caloric intake for the day. These social activities are essential and should by no means be pushed to the side for home eating. It's fair to assume you have had a night after a long day working that the last thing you want to do is spend a lot of the time in the kitchen making yourself a meal. Take-out is always an option, some even providing home delivery, but that is often a less healthy option than at-home cooking. Attempting to prepare your meals ahead of time, or batch cooking helps avoid forgetting lunch for work and usually avoids the late-night dash to the store, or a fast food chain.

If you are prone to snacking, having easily accessible healthy options is a must, but there are other tricks you can use if you feel like overindulging in snacks.

Brushing your teeth can mentally reset your brain, making eating anything directly after, less satisfying to taste but also affecting the cleanliness of your teeth - making you have to brush all over again. It is also essential that you are drinking water with and in between meals as sometimes our bodies will indicate we are hungry instead of indicating thirst.

It is vital to listen to our bodies if they indicate hunger, but often we misinterpret the signals it gives us; these techniques can help avoid excess eating. At no point should these techniques be used to replace meals.

Meal Preparations

So how can teachers avoid trying to make a last-ditch effort to put something healthy together for lunch as you are rushing out the door to school? If you can plan and prepare your food in advance, perhaps at the weekend, then you won't have to spend as much time each day cooking, which will free up more time for other activities and take out the guesswork of what there is to eat.

Preparing your meals in advance ensures you have a quick meal waiting for your lunch break or dinner each night or enables healthy snacking throughout the day. Most meals just need a simple reheat. Many people consume excess calories throughout the day by not having access to healthy eating options. When you cook your meals, you have complete control over not only the quantities of the food you are eating but the quality of the ingredients and components that go into the meal.

Consuming nutritious foods can be stigmatized due to the perception they are inaccessible and expensive. On the other hand, meal preparation can help you save money by allowing you to buy more significant quantities of ingredients and reduce your money on eating out. Frozen fruits and vegetables are available year-round and still hold critical nutrients. These options are also fantastic for meal prep as they are fast to prepare and last well when frozen.

If you want to gain more self-confidence in the kitchen, meal planning can be excellent for learning new cooking techniques. If like me, you can master a handful of simple but healthy dishes you can batch cook and eat over a few days. My current favorites are a vegetable filled chicken curry and spaghetti bolognaise. You could try making a simple soup in a slow cooker or roast chicken and vegetables (which you can repurpose as a salad the next day). You can also access freezer-friendly recipes that can be defrosted and reheated to make meal preps last longer.

Meal prepping can save you time, save you stress and help you to develop healthy eating patterns. Think about how impressed your students will be when you tell them what you're up to!

Meal prepping could also be a group activity to do with friends or coworkers. Whether a meal exchange or a cooking session, it turns it into something fun and allows you to learn more recipes. Sitting down one day and planning your meals is an excellent way to take control, and take positive steps toward becoming a healthier version of yourself.

Healthy Heart Habits

Cholesterol is a waxy substance your body uses to build cells and make vitamins and hormones. It is not inheritably bad and is a crucial part of human biology, but too much cholesterol can pose a problem. Your liver produces the cholesterol your body needs to continue these processes in your body however it is through the foods you eat you can start to amass excess cholesterol. Most animal products contain dietary cholesterol, unfortunately, most animal products are also high in trans fats, as well as saturated fats.

"These fats cause excess cholesterol production in the liver, that is, the bad kind of cholesterol. In turn, that leads to an increase in the overall level of cholesterol to a point where it's unhealthy, and dangerous" (Mayo Clinic, 2018).

The two types of cholesterol are LDL and HDL cholesterol, categorized as good or bad. As the amount of cholesterol in your blood increases, so does the risk to your health. High levels of cholesterol in your blood could lead to higher risks of heart-related health concerns.

"Too much of the wrong kind (LDL) or not enough of the good kind (HDL) increases the risk cholesterol will slowly build up in the inner walls of the arteries that feed the heart and brain" (Mayo Clinic, 2018).

That's why it's essential to have your cholesterol tested to know your levels. You can lower your cholesterol and enhance the health of your heart with only a few adjustments to your diet. Most of the saturated fats that contribute to an increase in your total cholesterol are found in red meat and full-fat dairy products. Low-density lipoprotein (LDL) cholesterol, also known as "bad" cholesterol, can be lowered by reducing the amount of saturated fat you consume. Trans fats, frequently found in margarine, cookies, crackers, and cakes purchased from a store, are occasionally stated on food labels as "partially hydrogenated vegetable oil."

Trans fats enhance total cholesterol levels. The Food and Drug Administration has decided to stop using vegetable oils that have been partially hydrogenated as of January 1, 2021. The levels of bad LDL cholesterol are unaffected by omega-3 fatty acids. However, they also have additional positive effects on cardiovascular health, including a reduction in blood pressure.

Salmon, mackerel, herring, walnuts, and flaxseed are all foods rich in omega-3 fatty acids. Soluble fiber can lower the amount of cholesterol absorbed into the bloodstream. Oatmeal, kidney beans, Brussels sprouts, apples, and pears are all foods containing soluble fiber. Whey protein, which may be found in dairy products, is suspected to be responsible for many of the reported health advantages of dairy.

According to several studies, using whey protein as a supplement brings down LDL cholesterol and total cholesterol while also bringing down blood pressure. Whey protein is readily incorporated into your regular diet and purchasable at many large chain grocery stores. Consider adding this and some of the aforementioned foods to maintain healthy cholesterol, and have regular checks with your doctor to ensure your levels are healthy.

Water

Water is your body's primary chemical component, accounting for approximately 50-70% of your total body mass. Water is essential to the health and function of every single cell, tissue, and organ in your body. For instance, water regulates your temperature, lubricates and cushions joints, eliminates waste through urination, perspiration, and bowel movements, and protects delicate tissues. For example, dehydration is the result of insufficient water and can lead to a lack of energy, headaches, and, in severe cases, death.

The National Academies of Sciences, Engineering, and Medicine in the United States concluded that men should drink approximately 15.5 cups, or 3.7 liters of fluids, daily. A daily total of approximately 11.5 cups, or 2.7 liters of fluid intake, is recommended for women. However, these numbers can change based on various things, such as exercise, pregnancy, or exposure to the individual's physical environment, whether it's hot or cold.

The average person gets about 20% of their daily fluid consumption from their diet, while the remaining 80% comes from beverages. Water makes up a high percentage of most beverages, including dairy products, fruit juices, and herbal teas, so even if you aren't drinking enough water specifically, it doesn't mean you aren't receiving the right amount of fluids you need during the day. Maintaining a regular intake of fluids between meals should be enough to maintain hydration, which can be represented in the smell and color of urine and not feeling thirsty.

Water is a crucial part of everyone's diet, enabling food to be correctly processed and your body to function properly. To implement more water intake buying a large water bottle for your day could be a start, alongside water intake apps and reminders. A popular item is water bottles with timestamps on the side to recommend the water intake over hour intervals. This could also be something to implement in your classroom, giving your students a small amount of water between periods. Although it is essential to remember the more fluid you intake, the more visits to the bathroom you will have throughout the day, making a routine that works best for you will be best to go along with the busy lifestyle of being a teacher.

Take Action

So the question is, what will you implement into your lifestyle to change your eating habits? Meal prepping lunches throughout the week can take away a lot of stress before work in the morning, alongside promoting healthy eating, heart health, and a healthy routine. Creating a productive way of putting together your meals minimizes the time it takes each day. Would you like to give it a shot? Here are a few simple steps to follow to get you started:

- Precook your proteins to add to salads or a carb dish
- Pre-cutting raw fruits and vegetables for snacks
- Boiling eggs for grab-and-go options
- Cook freezer-friendly meals to defrost and reheat like soups, pasta, or stir fry.
- Invest in some air-tight containers that can be stored in the fridge to have each food separated
- Label the meal preps with the date it was cooked to avoid eating spoiled foods.

Meal preparation also opens up the opportunity to try new recipes and cuisines. Look into some recipes that interest you or meals you always wanted to learn to make from scratch and implement them into your meal planning throughout the week. You can also utilize these new recipes to make healthy swaps, including eating foods focused on lowering your cholesterol. Try swapping out the type of pasta and bread you use, include more lean meats, and limit the number of eggs in your diet. Research parts of your diet you want to make a healthy switch to and find recipes that are freezable or easy to reheat to add to your meal preparations. Try adding more fruit and vegetables to your day by having prepared fruit in the fridge to grab and go or implementing a fruit snack break with your students in class.

Having a check-in with your general practitioner will allow you to understand what nutrients your body lacks or if there is an excess of certain things, including cholesterol, iron, or particular vitamins. They will also be able to advise you on food groups to avoid and what changes to make in your lifestyle. Regular check-ins with your doctor should be a generalized step to taking care of yourself.

Implementing a daily water goal can drastically improve a lot of facets of your life, including your skin and digestion, alongside mental and physical health; therefore, making a small goal could change a lot within your body. Try purchasing a large water bottle and mark out hourly goals. Having one large bottle a day should be an initial goal.

To achieve a healthy mindset you need a healthy lifestyle, and one of the first steps is understanding the foods you consume. These steps are just a few examples of what can be done daily to improve your overall mindset. Drink your water, consume healthy foods, and do whatever you can to make these processes easy to track and maintain.

Actions steps I will complete:

Chapter 3: Move your Body, Free your Mind

Participating in sport and physical activity can have a significant impact on improving mental health and reducing the symptoms of stress, anxiety, and depression. It has been suggested that engaging in physical activity on a regular basis can improve your mental well-being in a manner comparable to that of receiving psychotherapy! Exercise is a powerful first step on your journey towards improving your mental health and happiness.

When we talk about being consistent, it doesn't mean that you have to have a home gym or a membership to go to the gym regularly. You do not need a lot of expensive equipment or to spend a lot of money on exercise that makes you uncomfortable and leaves you less motivated than you were before you started. The movement has the potential to be enjoyable, motivating, and leave you feeling fulfilled. I've recently joined a local tennis club and I love it!

I am meeting new people, making friends and playing tennis two evenings a week. I've even entered a local beginners tennis league for a fun new challenge.

As teachers, we are often on the move throughout the day, from class activities to recess duty or walking to and from the staff room, all of which provides some exercise. However I would recommend that you start tracking your steps each day. Your smart phone probably does this automatically! 10,000 steps is a great goal to aim for each day. One handy tip is to get a few other teachers onboard and set up a daily 'walk and talk' routine each lunchtime to increase your steps for the day.

The Mental Benefits of Exercise

When discussing the effects of exercise on one's mental health, it is essential to consider the psychosocial factors at play. It has been demonstrated that regular exercise and physical activity through sports can distract from negative thoughts and both standard and clinical levels of anxiety and depression. So doing exercise actually makes you more happy!

Anxiety is one of the most prevalent mental health conditions, and it impacts a person's ability to focus, sleep and do daily duties. According to studies, exercising can lower anxiety levels, whereas not exercising is linked to increased levels of worry. Sometimes there is a correlation between anxiety and exercising, from being self-conscious about what you look like, worrying about stepping into the gym, or just internalized pressure of what other people will think.

Exercise needs to be done for yourself and should be a fundamental part of everyone's lives if they want to remain healthy. Whether it be a gym, an exercise class, a swimming pool, or a simple hike, everyone starts from somewhere, and the important thing is starting. If you're hesitant to walk in alone to your local sports club or yoga class, ask one of the teachers in your school to start it with you!

Move your Body

So now that we have covered the mentality behind exercising, it's time to get our bodies moving. Exercise can be simple, and it is about finding a way to enjoy your body moving; adding extra steps to your day by taking the stairs or walking to work where possible is a great initial goal.

Sometimes it feels like there aren't enough hours in the day, especially when, as a teacher, your work can blend from morning and the afternoon with grading papers and other planning and organizing. With family life, extra tasks you took on at school, commuting, cooking, caring for your pets or children and taking care of family members, it can be hard to find time for yourself!

You have enough happening in your day already, that sometimes implementing a new step in your routine can feel overwhelming.

But let's be frank here. Exercise doesn't have to involve jumping from machine to machine at the gym or going for a multi-mile run at dawn. Sure a small number of teachers probably do but that wouldn't be the choice for everyone!

Exercise should be adjusted to your individual needs. The way to start implementing exercise is by using the activities you already do daily. Try walking to and from work, and take any stairs on your journey. During lessons, try squatting down to talk to students, implement stretching or exercise-based brain breaks for yourself and your students, and walk between the buildings during your lunch break. It is all about adding a little extra movement to your day, which will develop your ability over time.

Suppose you're among the people who hate exercising; then it is about changing your mindset. There are a vast variety of ways to exercise and move your body. It's about finding movements that suit your body and lifestyle. You are more likely to fall out of habit and dread exercise if you do it in a way that you genuinely do not like.

That is why it is so crucial not only to find the right exercise for you but the right environment to allow yourself to be active and find some enjoyment in it. Like me playing tennis. I even enjoy playing in the rain!

If you find yourself using excuses not to leave the house to exercise, whether it be the weather, transport, or finances, there are easy ways to implement home routines that are just as effective as any gym workout.

HIIT (High-Intensity Interval Training) is a fast-paced workout that could be implemented into your morning for a 15-minute exercise that will leave your heart racing. Or, if a slower pace is your style, you could implement some yoga, which focuses on stretching out the body while still being short in time—with its slower pace, focusing on movements that focus on strength, balance, and flexibility, but most importantly, getting your body used to regular activity.

There are lots of free yoga videos you can try online. Many people find yoga relaxing and use it at all points during the day for relaxation.

Exercise could be turning on music and dancing around the house, running about with your children or pets, or even doing a fast-paced household cleaning session, anything that gets your body moving and your heart rate up.

Fast turnaround results are plastered everywhere next to the perfectly sculpted bodies suggesting if you just do this one workout routine or eat this particular meal plan, you can look just like them. Trends in the fitness industry are just as commonplace as any other industry allowing for a continuous stream of shifting ideals to be advertised in the mass media. From what time of the day is optimal to work out to cardio-based or weight-based workouts, fasting or non-fasting workouts are just examples of some areas that are always points of contention. That's why it is essential to look at everything with a grain of salt and talk to professionals about the best methods behind exercise, which could be nutritional advice or exercise physiology.

The ability to stay consistent and turn up for yourself regularly by exercising, reiterates your focus to improving your health and happiness. You are the only one who can make these changes for you, and exercising shows your body and mind that you are taking care of it, boosting your mental state and the likelihood of continuing to maintain this habit.

Group Exercise

People who suffer from anxiety or stress or any type, may benefit from the social aspect of physical activity, which can also serve as an outlet for these conditions. Not only does connecting with other people socially often deter anxiety symptoms, but it also allows people to interact in a rewarding situation, allowing the brain to connect this exercise to be a fun activity.

One of the significant benefits of finding a group or team exercise is the ability to show up and enjoy being a student again! If you show up for a gym class, your instructor has a program mapped out; if you are going to sports practice, you know you will be doing drills of some kind in preparation for a competition, or of course, if you are in a walking group, a predetermined route or hiking trail may already be planned ahead of time.

Regardless of the chosen group activity, it is worth considering an opportunity to exercise without having to plan it yourself. As a teacher, you map out your day when teaching, so why add another thing to outline in advance? With these professionally mapped-out exercises and classes, you just need to show up and enjoy it!

Depending on what's available locally, you might be able to find friends, groups, or teams to join to keep you motivated and accountable for showing up for yourself. Each season typically introduces a new sporting season bringing football, tennis, baseball, hockey, badminton and a never-ending list of team sports. Hiking, bike riding, indoor rock climbing, or utilizing a local gym are all activities that can be done year-round, often providing a place to exercise regardless of the weather. So regardless of the time of year, opportunities will be available to find a group within your community. This group work enables a sense of camaraderie and socializing and initiates potential friendships or relationships. These relationships can further push you to work harder, show up and stay consistent.

But suppose for some reason, it's not easy to join an in-person exercise group, such as a lack of availability, funding, or generalized access.

In that case, online communities are available to cater to like-minded people. These groups can be found on various websites or applications that can keep you motivated, connected, and guided through the process of introducing exercise into your life regularly.

Utilizing the varying groups in person or online can help you stay consistent, allowing you to familiarize yourself with others and create a social connection to the activity. The fun thing about group exercise is you are all there for the same reasons, regardless of your current level.

Subconsciously you will feel a competitive drive to dig deep in these group exercises, to feel part of the group and as though you did your part. This ingrained competitive nature helps you fight for your goals and push your team or group alongside you. It is not about pushing yourself past your limit or feeling guilty if you can't get as low or move as fast as others. They are focusing on themselves as you should also be.

The more you exercise, the more familiar your body will be with the movements, and you will be able to accomplish more. So regardless of your goal, consistency is the only way of accomplishing it.

Take Action

When trying out new exercise habits, it doesn't have to be a massive jump into the deep end. Take one step at a time. Try out one new class. Join one local club. When we exercise and do something that feels good for our bodies, maybe it's a new sport or class we have always wanted to try, it makes us feel physically and mentally well.

Try implementing a daily goal to hit a certain amount of steps a day or walk a specific walking route. Regular walking could drastically improve your overall well-being. Try finding a podcast or audiobook that you have wanted to dive into or make a playlist of music you love and try to walk for the duration of that program; often, you won't even notice how long you were out of the house.

From walking to other activities, it is up to you what you get involved in, what interests you, and what's available to you. Try looking into a team sport or exercise to enable the possibility of making a social connection while having fun and being physically active. Are there any local sports teams? What about local gyms? The first step recommended is to research your local community, see what is on offer around you, and try to implement at least one of the listed movements into your day-to-day activity.

There are plenty of questions to ask yourself to determine the best move for you to start your exercise journey. You are reflecting on your ability to maintain consistency with exercise habits and create your programs targeting our goals. Or are you more inclined to join a team or exercise class so you don't have to do the extra planning of a routine? There is also the discussion on financial availability regarding joining groups or gyms that has to be considered.

Try setting up a corner in your house with enough space to do some basic daily exercises, and try to remain consistent for a set amount of time to see if you can hit that goal. Maybe incorporate some pushups or sit-ups into your morning routine while you wait for your breakfast to cook. Find something you feel you can be consistent with, that works with your schedule.

Exercise doesn't have to be a chore; it can just be a regular part of your daily life. You are adding another step between home and school, allowing you to have a hobby that gets your body moving and reiterates the importance of taking care of yourself physically and psychologically. Start with small, extra steps, a few squats, and a plank for as long as possible. See if you can make a week out of one exercise, reflect on how it made you feel, rinse and repeat.

Actions steps I will complete:

Chapter 4: Eye of the Beholder

Finding confidence in yourself can be influenced by your appearance. It's not about looking like a celebrity or wearing a ton of makeup! It is about feeling good about yourself. It is about looking at yourself as the individual you are and loving what you see and who you are. It is about seeing your perceived flaws as beauty and finding the place within yourself to love your mind, body, and soul.

Finding a style that matches your personality and your profession might be easier for some than for others. Still, there are many ways to express yourself while dressing as a professional educator. There are better things to focus on than beauty. Still, feeling confident and comfortable in your skin, style, and being is worth focusing on, and sometimes focusing on looking good will help you feel better.

Finding Confidence

In mass media and online media, celebrities can be presented as perfect - with no flaws in their skin or body, reiterating a particular beauty standard. This has gone to crazy extremes. However, many celebrities are becoming wary of the use of photoshop and image editing software. Instead they are starting to embrace imperfections and advertise the idea that all bodies are beautiful.

In a massive cultural shift, there are now plus-size mannequins in stores and legs with cellulite all over social media. Fantastic! It is this embracing of your imperfections and understanding the beauty standard is a social construct that will alleviate any inner pressure you put on yourself and enable you to see yourself as what you are, beautiful.

Having people around you who build you up and make you feel comfortable within yourself will boost your overall self-worth and esteem. Sometimes we find ourselves around people who express their insecurities outwardly or may even point them out in us as individuals.

It is essential to recognize these people and their positions in your life. If you have people body shaming you in any way, they should not be allowed in a place to do so, and this includes family and friends.

Stand by your style, your shape, and your overall look with confidence. Not every style option is for everyone; you must stand by your choice. Wear your hair that way, dress that way, do your makeup that way and own it. As humans, we are constantly evolving. If you don't like it, there is no point in staying in one place regarding your style or image. Throughout our lives, fashions come and go. I do not doubt that there is a recognizable body ideal that has changed in your lifetime—making it pointless to have a particular body shape, style, and overall beauty standard. It's always a trend that will come and go.

Makeup is a helpful tool to adjust how you look by utilizing face, eye temporarily, and lip shades to amplify your face. Makeup used to be a female targeted industry, but as time continues, men are more publicized in makeup, becoming more normalized in society.

Whatever makes you as an individual feel comfortable with your appearance and is within the policy of your school can be used to make you feel more comfortable and express yourself in your working environment. Although makeup needs to be recognized as a temporary option to finding confidence within yourself, it is a tool to enhance and express your individuality. It can be fun, similar to the use of accessories or nail polish. Sometimes even making time in your day to do a little self-care - from painting your nails a new color to enjoying a DIY facial at home, can add peace and help our minds to slow down and relax.

Confidence is about understanding and accepting who you are and what you look like and taking steps to take care of yourself to promote overall self-esteem. There are many ways to express your individuality, and continue to provide yourself with the opportunity to build your self-esteem. Embracing this individuality also shows your students that being different is cool and empowers them to express themselves in their way.

Wardrobe and clothing

Your clothing says a lot about you. Your appearance is one of the first statements you can make before meeting someone, and how you dress takes up most of the focal point. Your clothing can paint a picture of your overall personality and style and enables you to express yourself however you want to be perceived or perceive yourself.

Your style can be whatever you want it to be, from polished and conservative to the brightest of colors, and you could make statements about causes you are passionate about, show off your humor, or even express your emotions. From dressing to your body's shape to your age to colors that match your complexion, it is entirely interchangeable for each individual.

Teachers usually follow a particular dress code in their school to maintain a level of professionalism. But this does not have to limit how you express yourself. Enjoying the clothes you wear can boost your confidence and help you feel happy.

Clothing can indeed change your mood and change how people will perceive you.

You wear a suit at a coffee shop and sit on your phone, and people will think you're doing business. Bright colors make you friendly and approachable, and darker ones make you more solitary. These are perceptions of other people, but sometimes confidence can be how you think you are making other people see you.

You see it all the time with social media influencers wearing head-to-toe designers in hopes people will see them as wealthy and successful. Some of the world's most affluent people wear the same predictable clothes every day - think of Steve Jobs! It is all about what message you want to convey to others in how you dress.

The first step is to take inventory of what clothes you have in your closet today. Do you have any clothes in your closet that you haven't worn in over 12 months? One evening this week, go through all your clothes and put everything you haven't worn in over 12 months together. It might be time to donate these clothes to a local charity shop. If you don't wear them, they don't need to be in your wardrobe! You'll help other people and declutter your wardrobe at the same time.

Clothing is expressive, showing you are a person that has been determined.

What about utilizing this to enable yourself to explore your creativity also? Trying new styles, buying second hand at a thrift shop, and upcycling, maybe even doing your alterations. Make it fun, do some crafts, tie dye or bleach, and design exciting prints. Make it a point to continue to let your wardrobe speak volumes without you having to say a word.

Though there are some limitations to being an educator, your school has a dress code strictly for its teachers. However, there are still many ways to work your personality into the dress code and express yourself. Comfortable yet flattering clothes are an excellent first step. You will always feel more comfortable in clothes that make you feel good. Try accessorizing your style with jewelry. Whether it be rings, necklaces, or earrings, there are so many ways to express different moods, holidays, or themes for your classroom in a fun way.

Try a new color shirt, try some fun earrings, or a new hat. Anything can be shifted into making your clothing fun, unique, and a perfect portrayal of you.

Hair, Skin, and Teeth

Maintaining your physical appearance is directly linked to more self-confidence and higher self-esteem, but this should not be limited to the clothes you wear but should be a part of your daily care routine.

Your hair is a simple yet effective way to boost your confidence, change your style, and express yourself. From cutting to styling and dying, your hair is in a constant state of change. Taking care of your hair indicates to others that you care about yourself and your presentation. Messy unkept hair can show that your consideration for yourself and your presentation to others isn't a priority. We have spoken about how you present yourself as a direct reflection of how you feel about yourself or generalized internal feelings, and this is the same with hair left unkempt. Though our hair is often styled appropriately for the intended activity for the day, it could be a fun thing to switch up. Have a day where you take yourself to a salon or barber and get a fresh do, allowing for the added extras of a shampoo, blowdry, or beard trim. It can boost the confidence you need while also making yourself presentable.

Your skin's dullness, chapped lips, or thinning hair could be seen as your diet lacking particular components to keep these areas of your body healthy. These are problems that can harm your self-esteem as well as your overall skin health. So, how do you regain your hair's luster or that youthful glow? Natural dietary supplements may provide the solution you seek. Vitamin-infused skincare products for your skin and hair are widely available today. But keep in mind that they are not all equally efficient. Biotin, along with vitamins A, B, C, D, and E, is among the most beneficial vitamins for skin health and hair growth. These vitamins can work wonders for your skin and hair if taken in the proper amounts and at regular intervals. Their antioxidant properties can do wonders to restore your skin's suppleness and your hair's growth and shine.

Skincare can be typically overlooked by many people, including generalized washing to routines that incorporate products to better the appearance of your skin. Caring for your skin has been linked to many benefits and studies associated with generalized skincare and an individual's wellbeing.

A 2020 study was conducted to determine how over-the-counter skin care products affect women's quality of life. The effects of the 28-day facial skin care routine were monitored. Using commercially available products made to improve elasticity, firmness, and hydration and to correct age and sun-related skin color changes were used in the study. After using the product for a while, panelists said that their skin made them feel more confident, happy, and proud of their appearance. Improvements in the self-image and self-competence subdomains were caused by changes in how the individuals felt about themselves, like how they felt about their physical appearance, how confident they felt, and how well they could take care of themselves.

In general, busy individuals are more likely to spend less time thinking about their health. As a parent to a young child doing their skincare routine during the day, as seen in the above study, allows them time to do something just for themselves. This enables them to prioritize themselves for a short time every day, taking care of their appearance.

As seen in the study, new mothers felt more like they had been before becoming a parent, having put themselves first for a moment to take care of themselves and not someone else genuinely.

This resulted in many of the participants in the study feeling more confident in themselves and happier with their overall appearance.

This study is an excellent example of how skin care can make a noticeable change to your appearance and willingness to take care of yourself. And this works for elementary school teachers too! Having the time to take care of yourself in ways like a skincare routine enables you to have that time just to yourself.

It doesn't have to be an extensive or expensive routine. Implementing something as simple as a moisturizer and sunscreen will improve the look or feel of your skin and its health. Sunscreen helps protect the skin from the sun, which ages our skin and can cause severe life-threatening cancers if exposed for too long. So while we might want to avoid those wrinkles and sun spots, there are important reasons to include sunscreen into your everyday regime. Like your hair, missing vitamins and minerals will show in your skin's overall appearance, tone, and elasticity. Over-the-counter vitamins or meals, including lots of vitamins and antioxidants, will help maintain your skin's youthful glow.

Teeth

Dental care should be a regular step in your regime; from wanting those pearly whites to wanting minty fresh breath, we should brush our teeth twice a day. Besides waiting to abolish morning breath and the smell of your lunch tuna sandwich, brushing your teeth is essential to avoid the need for a trip to the dentist. Most people have experienced a toothache and know the pain of having a throbbing in their jaw. This sensation needs to be treated by a dentist if it persists, and this can become expensive. Preventative care of the teeth to avoid any build-up, decay, or pain is through, you guessed it, brushing and flossing your teeth. Regular checkups are also necessary to ensure that everything is healthy and that no new problems appear in your oral health.

Take Action

Taking care of your body is not limited to exercise, and taking care of something as simple as your hair, skin, and teeth can make a difference. The way we dress can make you feel comfortable not only physically and based on the environment you are in, but also that matches your style. Putting together a few go-to outfits that are a good mixture of streetwear, workwear, and dinner wear will help you feel comfortable within your options. Cleaning your wardrobe to avoid excess guilt or choices associated with picking your outfit options will streamline the process.

Tossing your hair up in a simple bun or ponytail or running your hands through it before you get to work might be an easy way to prepare for the day, but do you take pride in this? Take five minutes of your morning to brush through and apply a little product or take a supplement to encourage healthy hair, skin, and nails. Men should keep beards trimmed and maintained. Some products to hold them in place would also be beneficial. Try booking an appointment for a new style or just a fresh cut. Consider a new color or maybe make a big change. It will grow back!

Lastly, but equally important, a daily routine will help you maintain regular dental hygiene and primary skin care. Try to make sure every day after breakfast and before bed, you brush your teeth and floss. This is the most basic of dental hygiene, any additional steps such as regular dentist visits would also be advised, though can take more time and planning. In addition to dental hygiene, a basic skincare routine can start making massive changes in the appearance of your skin. Cleansing, moisturizing, and using sunscreen daily will help prevent sun damage and clogged pores. This can also deter acne.

If you have acne on your shoulders or back, another tip is to not wash out your hair conditioner onto these areas, without rinsing them thoroughly after. Hair conditioner left on these areas after you shower can clog up your pores and affect your skin quality. So rinse your body thoroughly afterwards, or rinse your hair out without allowing your hair conditioner to run onto your upper body.

Remember, these steps are not just to accomplish an outward appearance shift but to make you feel more confident within yourself and how you present outwardly to others. These are mere steps in finding confidence within yourself and will show that you are important enough for the primary care of yourself.

Actions steps I will complete:

Chapter 5: Technology

Technology changes incredibly quickly. We've moved from snail mail to instant messaging, video calls, and video conferencing. Most people have a multitude of ways they can be contacted 24/7, anywhere in the world! There will always be both positives and negatives with technology.

Even the Internet itself has changed. Its early years—which, historically speaking, are still recent—were spent as a static network built to transfer a small amount of data between two terminals. It was a repository for knowledge where the content was only created and updated by skilled programmers.

Today, however, enormous amounts of data are uploaded and downloaded over this electronic behemoth. Most of the content on social media we have created ourselves. During the 1980s and 1990s. The Internet experienced rapid expansion; it was no longer a government-run endeavor and had grown to become the largest computer network in the world.

The emergence of Web 2.0 in the first decade of the twenty-first century was a revolution in and of itself. It encouraged the development of social media and other interactive, crowd-based communication tools. The Internet was a sophisticated multidisciplinary tool that allowed people to create content, communicate with one another, and even escape reality. It was no longer just about exchanging information. Today, we can send data instantly from one end of the planet to the other, create online presentations, participate in parallel "game worlds," and share our true selves through text, images, sound, and video.

With the constant shift in technological advancement, from the expansion of the internet reaching all over the globe and opening up opportunities for connection and knowledge, it also brings forth security and privacy problems, scammers, and sometimes questionable data or highly targeted clickbait headlines, presented as 'facts' by people with higher agendas.

We began to compare ourselves with others, with constant shifting trends thrown at us from every angle, and suddenly, our smartphones are attached to us at all times. What if someone can't contact us? That would be a disaster, right? Well maybe not!

Though there are both positive and negative aspects to the internet and this growth in technology, it's important to use this positive side of technology to grow and learn, and it has many ways to benefit our lives - from same day virtual consultations with a doctor to talking to your grandchild in Australia over a video call.

Social Media

58.4% of the world's population uses social media, and the average daily usage is 2 hours and 27 minutes (Chaffey, 2022). Social media allows international and local communication by sharing life experiences, photographs, dating, and connections. Facebook, Instagram, Twitter, and TikTok are just some of the examples of successful apps that entertain billions of people per year (Eneix, 2021). These apps can be used for many forms of entertainment and communications, allowing people to maintain a connection consistently. Though many benefits can be found, there are always disadvantages.

Although not explicitly connected, social media usage can link to adverse mental health conditions with consistent comparisons relating to body image, self-esteem, and play on people's insecurities.

For teachers also, it can be awkward to get a friend request from a student who found your social media profile online. A quick private chat, to let them know that you only use social media for their friends, and the student is your student - not your friend, usually clears up any confusion.

I believe that teachers should be able to have social media accounts under their own names - and not try to hide online in case a student finds them. Teachers are allowed to have lives too!

There are teacher specific forums and groups that can provide useful support and resources, if you look in the right places, that can be very helpful.

Virtual cleanup

As an elementary school teacher you don't need to stress managing your email inbox! Organizing your email inbox can be difficult, but there are some great tools out right now to help you make sense of it all. Some emails will just need a quick response and others might require more in depth responses; with these organizational resources at the ready (and blocked notifications!), managing those incoming messages becomes much easier!

There are some great ways to organize your emails so you can get rid of the ones that aren't relevant while still being able to send and receive important messages. One way, for example, would be creating folders in an account with specific names like "important" or "family." Then put all subscriptions into these designated areas instead; it will make tracking them easier as well!

Consider adjusting your notifications settings to notify priority emails and ensure all messages are silenced throughout the night. This way, you'll have more time for sleep!

The average person has over 100 apps on their phone. And with all of this storage capability, we often don't realize how much data is taking up space - unneeded photos and videos from old occasions you don't need; notifications for things like social media sites or emails that never get read because there's no need to check them at any given time. Deleting these unused applications will not only clear out unneeded data but also make room in your device so storage isn't an issue.

You can also create folders on your phone, and group different types of apps together. One folder could have school related apps. One folder could have social media apps. The next folder, travel related apps.

You can change the notifications for each of your apps, from temporarily disabling them for a set period to entirely removing them from your device.

We all have that one app which just won't leave us alone, no matter how much we try to ignore it. I know for me it's the incessant notifications from my phone telling me "you haven't updated this in a while," or some other similar message trying hard to get your attention! I'm sure most people can relate...

So go ahead and change the notification on your apps. Do you really need an audio alert when someone leaves a comment on a picture? One handy tip is to remove your most used apps from your phone, and instead only use a computer, laptop, or another internet-connected device to check in on their social media. This can drastically reduce the time spent scrolling in a day.

Screen Time

As teachers, our days are filled with teaching, planning, printing, organizing, and taking care of children, on top of any extra activities we undertake throughout the school day and after hours. Utilizing the time outside the school day is essential for bettering your health and happiness. There are various ways to disconnect from social media and boost your overall mental health associated with using technologies and devices regularly.

On your smartphone, you can determine how much of the screen time is spent on each app.

Screen time isn't inherently bad. Using our smart devices to contact friends or family, stay up to date on what's happening in the world, and watch one or two funny cat videos is entirely OK in today's world.

Assessing your screen time can help determine what apps are consuming too much of your time. If you are scrolling on social media and suddenly notice the sun has gone down, or you missed a television program you were excited to watch, or suddenly it's time for bed, maybe it's time to reassess your priorities.

There are many apps specifically to teach and help individuals to grow, from podcasts, audiobooks, language learning, skill building, and education. All bettering your time spent on your device and allowing you to build your knowledge. These apps can also leave you feeling happy and content with what you have consumed. I would definitely recommend audio apps, podcasts and audiobooks. I love to listen to an audiobook while on a one hour walk doing my daily 10,000 steps.

It's not all bad

As teachers, we are constantly introduced to new technology. Going from a chalkboard to a smart integrated board that can play videos and map out lessons digitally is a huge step in technology in the classroom. Some schools utilize tablets or iPads to complete classes, and IT (Information Technology), typing, and basic computer use are integrated into schooling.

So, technology cannot be avoided in the classroom, and depending on your school, it may be deemed necessary, so it's time to find apps that help you as a teacher better your activities, planning, and lessons. Although access to these options may be limited depending on your school's funding and the ability to get technology in schools, some apps can be used professionally to track the class progression used as study tools or quiz apps that are fun for students.

Being able to show students an educational film, show them instructional videos, or just incorporate the many different features into the teacher's planned lessons allows for different types of learning to be undertaken. Technology has enabled more diversified lessons, with access to an infinite pool of resources, instruction, and ideas to make class fun. These same technologies have allowed rural schools to access the same quality of classes and subjects that those in more developed cities have. Whether it be by access to the information or the teachers themselves via the internet.

Throughout this book I have suggested various apps from sleep trackers to step counters to track aspects of your life that, if improved, can improve your health both physically and mentally.

Drawing a form line between the apps that aid your mental health and those that burden you and gradually take time away from what matters is essential to allow yourself to get the maximum benefit from your smartphone. .

Take Action

You didn't have to read this chapter to know that technology can distract us and waste our time! We are all guilty of spending just a little too much of our spare time on our phones or watching television, perhaps even procrastinating a work task or avoiding physical and social interaction.

Understanding the amount of time spent on specific apps and what you are doing on them is crucial to understanding what you are committing your time to. Are you constantly spending hours on a social media page, not finding any worth in the content you are consuming? Maybe it's time to lower that screen and dedicate the time you have towards a new skill, a hobby, or something you have been procrastinating. So the first step is to track the time you spend watching TV and on digital devices each day.

Perhaps you have not yet got around to organizing your notifications, apps, emails, and photographs. Utilizing a small amount of time can help you clean up your phone. And don't get distracted by social media while you're doing this!

Choose one project to work on today, whether it be the cleanup of your email, the removal of unused apps on your phone, the cleanup of your google drive files, or simply checking your screen time to see how much time you spend using your various electronic devices.

If you spend more than one hour per day on social media, you should think about what you want to get out of that time and what you can do to change how you spend your time online. Do you realize that you spend so long on Facebook every day? Are you looking at the content or just scrolling through it? Additionally, how do you feel as a result of the information? Sometimes, all that is required is some quiet introspection on how these behaviors impact your mood, followed by a step toward ending the never-ending social media scrolling. Think about removing these apps from your device so you can only use them through your web browser.

When it comes to cleaning up and reducing the amount of your digital and online presence, you have a wide variety of options available to you. Choosing just one easy action could bring you a world of relief from your anxious thoughts. In a world as chaotic as that of teachers, the last thing we need is an additional source of stress. Therefore, the time has come to take action and concentrate on determining which aspect of our lives is more important to prioritize our timeline or free time.

Actions steps I will complete:

Chapter 6: Household Organization

Making changes in your life can feel super intimidating, but it's important to remember that starting small and breaking these tasks into smaller pieces will make them more manageable.

It's always easier to give up when you're feeling overwhelmed by an unorganized home. And as busy elementary school teachers, the last thing we want to happen is to go home and feel more stressed when we see a ton of clutter everywhere. But this doesn't have to happen. There are handy methods for decluttering and organizing so that it doesn't feel like too much work, especially if we take short breaks from and just organize one space at a time over a week or to.

There may be some therapeutic benefits associated with decluttering. For instance, Belk and colleagues discovered that people have a more positive perception of themselves and their surroundings after decluttering at least some of the items in their homes.

We all have a natural tendency to want more money and possessions, but what many people don't realize is that simplifying your life can actually make you happier. And this includes teachers! It has been proven by studies done on simple living which show how rearranging one's schedule or giving up certain habits will improve not only their physical health but also mental wellbeing as well!

Decluttering your house every few months can be very rewarding. Some examples of such habits include spring cleaning, storing your winter clothes and replacing them with your summer wardrobe, and doing a fall declutter after the summer.

Individuals can attribute clutter to memories associated with items. But eventually these begin to pile up in a mass of unsorted mementos. We;ve all got that one drawer full of random items right?

Sometimes it's about reassessing the importance of this physical object with the memory and coming to a decision. Once this decision has been made that the item is important it's about finding the appropriate space for it.

A Tidy Home, a Tidy Mind

Having clutter and general mess in your house does not help your peace of mind. It's easy to collect random stuff that you hold onto for whatever reason every time you try to tidy the house. It's time to finally address this clutter and disarray and clear your physical and mental space. It's easy to blame the chaos on a busy schedule or lack of time, but in most cases, it's just not prioritizing the area around you and the impact the space has on your wellbeing.

There are many psychological reasons behind having a messy space. Maybe this habit also overflows into your classroom, car, or wallet? We are talking about the clutter that will always be sorted "one day" or is hidden away to be avoided.

According to Teri Lynn Mabbitt, the various forms of clutter can be divided into four categories. Clutter, in the technical sense, refers to anything that reduces available space and adds to the overall scarcity of storage space.

Changes in a person's life, such as the birth of a new child, the loss of a loved one, a move, or anything else that has thrown one's life out of whack, can also contribute to the accumulation of clutter in their living space.

Lack of time management and life organization, which refers back to the mentality of "I'll do it later," is another system that contributes to the accumulation of clutter. All of these categories are examples of aspects of life that we as humans will experience at some point or another.

The Main Culprits

Consumerism has become an epidemic in our society, and we are constantly being marketed to by advertisements from brands that only want us for their money. With all this advertising comes the idea of consumption--the more you buy, the better off your life will be. But this approach generates a lot of waste. Sometimes consumers can get caught up with buying something to get the adrenaline rush, but then the item gets added to other things in a drawer, cupboard, garage, or wherever it may be.

Documentation can be a problematic area to sort through, and they are often stored in complete disarray with no organization or filing system. As a teacher, you can provide many resources, including lesson plans and craft and learning activities from your home. Your equipment, from stamps and stickers to templates and books, can become disorganized if not paid attention to. Suppose you notice you don't have a filing system to separate personal and professional documents. This makes it easy to lose essential forms or documents, including your birth certificate or bank statements. So it is time to start putting it all in order.

Make the switch from getting physical bills mailed to your address to get digitized bills or statements straight to your email. Using the steps in the previous chapter, you can set rules to make a folder within your email that directly receives all funds, and you will get notified of them. Besides bills, scanning or getting digitized receipts allows you to avoid excess paper that needs to be sorted by hand and cut down on paper usage.

Wardrobes can be filled with junk that is and never organized or looked at very often. Ensure each item in your wardrobe has a purpose.

Start by taking everything out of your wardrobe and going through one item at a time. Make up three piles of items you want to keep, donate and throw away and make yourself reflect on the fit, quality, and how often you use the item.

We all have a stash of 'someday' clothes. Clothes we will be able to fit in, feel confident in, have an occasion for, someday. These clothes are just a constant reminder of a different time and a different situation. It's time to start taking out those clothes and organizing your wardrobe to make the clothes you do reach for more accessible. Add additional storage to your wardrobe to allow further organization, such as hooks, bins, containers, and extra racks when placing your items back.

Making everything easier to access will help reiterate what you have and avoid purchasing items that are already in your household. We are all guilty of a run to the store for something we forgot, but already have stashed at the back of a cupboard or inside a miscellaneous drawer.

Do you have a place to store all those Christmas items you have? Is there a mass of broken baubles, lights that don't work, or a figure of Santa with a missing limb? Out of sight, out of mind is an easy way to manage these occasion-based items.

The garage always ends up as a dumping ground for the items that don't have a place, and for some reason, you're not willing to let go of them. Gym equipment, the kid's old bikes, your high school prom photos, whatever it may be, it should not just sit in a box accumulating over time. It needs to be addressed.

Simple Systems and Home Cleaning

Homes get messy over time. It's just a part of day-to-day life. To ensure your house is clean and organized, I would recommend you designate time each week to clean your home. Maybe it's a Sunday morning. Or a Monday evening after school.

Although a simple step like wiping all the table counters or organizing the mail might seem insignificant, small actions like these can have big positive effects in how we feel at home. It's not about a last-ditch effort to tidy before guests come or someone comes to do work on your house. It is about decluttering, organizing and tidying for your peace of mind.

Spring cleaning is when you deep clean your household, cleaning the closets and various storage places in your home of clutter, junk, and any dust or grime that has built up since the last spring clean.

Having a routine for cleaning will help you keep in control of any clutter or mess. If you have multiple people in your household, are they pulling their weight regarding the upkeep?

Marie Kondo revolutionized the idea of decluttering and maintaining a clean space, with her philosophy gaining traction across the internet. Her method recommends organizing by category rather than by location, starting with clothing and working through books, papers, miscellaneous items, and finishing with sentimental items. Discard anything that no longer makes you happy, and only keep things that speak to your heart.

This philosophy appeals to people worldwide not only because it is a useful method but also because it emphasizes the value of mindfulness, reflection, and looking ahead.

Having suitable places for temporary or seasonal items such as swimming equipment or holiday decorations enables all the items to be stored together easily. So you won't be missing the star for the top of the Christmas tree or your left flipper when you're going snorkeling!

One of the most popular services for busy homeowners is weekly house cleaning for a couple of hours each week and lawn and garden maintenance during the summer. While it might sound a little odd, many teachers who hired a cleaner for a few hours each week loved the massive difference it made in their quality of life. Not only did they walk into a clean house each day after school, it saved them hours of cleaning each week - which they hated doing anyway! It is worth researching house cleaners in your area to check how much they charge. See if you can get a recommendation from friends who use this service already.

Take Action

So what aspects of decluttering and cleaning resonate with you? Do you have a room that you rarely walk into, because it's too disorganized and stresses you out? Maybe you have an overflowing wardrobe? An abundance of shoes you rarely wear?

Often it is just getting started that's the hardest part. But once you get started, you will be able to focus on the task and feel proud when you start to see a cleaner and more organized house. Try picking just one category of things to go through, maybe something you have been putting off for a while, and see where that takes you.

No one's home is perfect, and it is not about perfection. But starting up a regular daily or weekly set of things to do around the house is an excellent first step to routinely cleaning and maintaining your house. Try to wipe your benches after every meal is cooked. Wash your dishes daily, change your sheets once a week, and slowly start introducing the tasks to become a regular part of your schedule.

Maybe you feel you have been consistent with a daily and weekly cleaning routine, and now it's time you consider decluttering the crevices where you stash your things to address at another time.

If you can outsource some of your tasks around the house to minimize the household duties, it could be worthwhile to test it out. If decluttering is becoming overwhelming, or you just need assistance, physical companies and online programs can help you through the organizational step of your life. It's worth looking into what's available in your local area or chatting to your neighbors about what services they use. After all, what's the harm in doing some research and drawing conclusions yourself?

It's time to prioritize the space you have around you. Your home should be your safe space, not a place that brings you anxiety. These simple steps will get you started on having a clean stress free home. These methods can be used anywhere, from your car to the classroom or anywhere you feel chaotic with clutter. It's time to eliminate the excess so you can appreciate what truly matters.

Actions steps I will complete:

Chapter 7: Stress

The word "stress" has been reduced to just another buzzword in our society, but what does it mean for you? Stress can be damaging both physically and mentally. If handled incorrectly then this can affect your physical health as well mental state of mind which could lead into more serious problems.

It can be difficult for teachers to maintain work-life balance. Maintaining a healthy life is essential for mental well being and can help with the stress of teaching!

Stress is a part of life, but it's up to you how much pressure builds inside. The key isn't eliminating all your worries and concerns; rather learn what tools work best for lowering and dealing with that stress each day.

Habits and Stress

One way of preventing and reducing stress is to create new healthy habits. Our overall well-being is something that is incredibly important. Introducing better habits into your life, like drinking water every day and exercising regularly will help you feel healthier in general as well as give more time for things important to YOU!

So let's talk about stress-reducing habits that can be very useful for elementary school teachers.

There are little things you do every day that add up to make a big difference! For example, drinking water can help keep dehydration at bay so it doesn't affect other parts of our bodies like brain function; staying physically active helps us stay energized throughout each workday while maintaining healthy weight loss goals if we have them - plus exercise has been shown as an effective way for reducing anxiety symptoms too.

Try utilizing meal prepping, enabling you to make a habit of cooking your meals at home and having easy options for grab-and-go situations. Try drinking more water and making it a habit to have a glass every hour. Make your bed when you wake up, or create another morning routine that allows you to have a calm morning.. This might be waking up to a new softer alarm, taking deep breaths, drinking a glass of water before you get up, or allowing yourself some time to journal. Maybe your perfect morning is playing with your pets, following your daily five minute vitamins and skincare routine or reading the headlines in the online newspaper.

These routines allow your body and mind to settle as you begin each day. Similar structures and ideas can be implemented throughout the day to allow you to make more calming routines that enable you to have a stress-free experience.

Setting Boundaries to Reduce Stress

Clear boundaries can greatly benefit our mental and emotional health. Having clear boundaries also helps our physical health. They allow us to care for ourselves before others, and can actually benefit both parties. Like an inflight emergency procedure, you must put a mask on yourself before helping others. The willingness to assist other people is typically a significant component of our personalities; after all, who doesn't want to be the person who helps other people?

As educators, one of our primary responsibilities is to assist our students. This aspect of our work is typically one of the primary motivating factors that led us to pursue a career in education in the first place. Because of these traits, you might find yourself trying to please everyone. People who are always willing to say yes to other people's requests, regardless of how it might affect them personally, are known as "people pleasers." Being a person who helps and appeases others are two entirely different things to strive for.

Some people actively bring stress into our lives, constantly involved in drama, using us as a constant support network regardless of our mental capacity for dealing with their drama and emotions. These people often don't consider our feelings, our ability, or what is on our plate as individuals, using the fact that we seek to please people.

The way to avoid being used this way is to set healthy boundaries for yourself and others regarding how they communicate or interact with you. To some, this might be a scary concept. The idea of saying no can often be intimidating, especially when dealing with other people who have come to be used to walking all over you.

Acknowledging people that use you or are constantly bringing you down is essential for understanding your self-worth. Not everyone will treat you how you deserve, nor will they always be there when you need them in return.

Setting boundaries allows you to show others how to respect you in areas including your space, needs, personality, values, and possessions. Boundaries also enable you to distribute your resources effectively and accurately, such as your time, money, and your physical and emotional energy.

You want to prioritize what is essential for you first, so setting boundaries allows you to follow these passions or past-times with ease, without stressing about other people demanding your time in a relationship that seems to mostly benefit the other person.

Those within your inner circle and support system should be understanding of your boundaries. No one should put anyone else in the position of feeling as though their boundaries have been breached or questioned by another person, especially a friend.

Finding these relationships that respect your boundaries, will create a relationship out of mutual respect and understanding.

Support Systems

Having a strong support system in place is one of the best ways to live life fully and be happy. Research has shown that higher levels of well-being, improved coping mechanisms, as well as longer healthier lives can all result from having close friends or family members who care about you deeply!

It has also been demonstrated that having a support system lowers stress, depression, and anxiety. We require a support system that will be there for us in times of need.

A support system is a network of individuals who can offer you either emotional or practical support. When you have a support system, you have people you can turn to when you need them most. It implies that there are people you can rely on whenever you find yourself in challenging circumstances. This could be anything from picking you up at the airport to offering advice to you about a difficult situation you're dealing with, at home or at school.

Having a group of people around you who support your overall wellbeing can be a gamechanger. Support systems can be people from your sports team, parents, school colleagues, lifelong friends, or siblings. They can uplift you and support you. Often these people may exist in your life without you recognizing them as a support system but merely as a friend or family member you feel you can be honest with and communicate with, without any judgment or discomfort.

Support systems are very important in mental and physical wellbeing, and often, they are close enough to you that they know when you begin to withdraw, get stressed, or have other matters pop up in your life that you might not feel like sharing.

These systems do not have to be made up of family members or people you would associate with 'being close to.' Many out there wouldn't consider their parents or siblings as being a supportive unit in their life which is okay.

The importance of having these people who care about your overall well-being is knowing that they have your back and bring happiness to your life. Spending time with people who make you happy makes you feel happy within your group and more positive toward yourself.

Mental and Physical Health Check-ins

A lot of individuals hold onto stress relating to their health. Having semi-regular checkups with your general practitioner allows you to get some peace of mind about your overall health. If you are a generally healthy person with no underlying conditions that need consistent treatment, you might not visit the doctor's office much at all.

A recommended yearly check-in with blood work can help determine if your diet is getting the proper nutrients in your body. This can be as quick as a fifteen to twenty-minute appointment that can bring about some peace of mind and minimize your stress about anything you may be concerned about.

Even if the doctor indicates something to be fixed or altered, this needs to be seen as a positive, not a negative. Getting a grasp on your physical and mental health is always important. While sometimes that might mean using medication, adding an extra vitamin to your daily diet, or some changes in your regular lifestyle, this is a positive step towards improving your overall health

This also goes hand in hand with other specialists you may need to visit, depending on your situation. Regular dental checkups and cleaning can help you stay informed about the health of your teeth and gums and alleviate any stress you might have regarding dental hygiene.

Visiting the optometrist to get your glasses prescription redone and your eyes rechecked are all helpful steps that should be done regularly. Again, early intervention is the best if any abnormalities are found. This includes dental and optical preventions and treatment. You aren't always going to the doctor or specialist because you think something is wrong. Sometimes it is just a good thing to be 100% healthy and go for a health check to double check there is nothing you're not aware about going on!. All areas of our lifestyle impact the health of our bodies, and the best we can do is regularly check-in with our doctor and ensure we are in tip-top shape.

We are in a world where everything is constantly changing and moving. We are encouraged to have a work ethic, family, and friends, go out regularly, exercise, continue learning, and have well looked after homes. Actually, sometimes the best thing we can do for ourselves is to give ourselves a break!

Stop moving, stop having so many plans, constant deadlines or a crazy to do list. Our lives are not meant to be a never-ending run from task to task. We need to find the time for ourselves to sit down, relax and reflect. Time to do nothing!

This can be daily, and this could be once a week. It could fit into whatever time you consider to be free. This time needs to be for yourself, doing what you love and taking care of yourself—having a bubble bath, reading a good book, taking yourself out to lunch, going for a slow-paced walk in your favorite park, or lying on the lounge all day binge-watching your favorite TV show. It is about giving your mind, body, and soul a reset.

The hard part about these days off is feeling the need to do something. Some people can grow restless in need of doing something. This can be an excellent time to get back into hobbies or things that will make you happy but won't cause stress. Rest days are not the days to start DIYing a kitchen renovation or to volunteer for a new project.

Let yourself be able to spend the time doing nothing, and sometimes this might be when your body acknowledges how tired it is or your mind finally settles into how you genuinely feel. This is an integral part of the process. Allowing yourself to feel the way you think and accept it and giving yourself the time to nurture those feelings as the good or the bad they may be.

Meditation and Mindfulness

"A growing body of research has shown that practicing mindfulness can help reduce stress and anxiety, improve attention and memory, and promote self-regulation and empathy" (How to Manage Stress with Mindfulness and Meditation, 2021).

An increasing range of studies demonstrating that mindfulness lowers stress and anxiety, enhances attention and memory, and fosters self-regulation and empathy has contributed to mindfulness's popularity. Usually consistency is needed because the results take time to manifest, but mindfulness can really help to improve the quality of your life.

Despite the growing popularity of mindfulness, a common misconception about the practice is that it requires participants to empty their minds, engage in brief periods of sleep, or enter trances. Beginners frequently experience difficulties falling asleep, feeling comfortable, battling challenging thoughts or emotions, becoming bored or distracted, and waking up. According to experts, the process should ideally be practiced in a group setting under the guidance of an instructor.

Thousands of free online guided mindfulness and meditation apps or videos will allow you to feel deeply relaxed. These exercises don't have to be done in a specific place, just somewhere where you can focus on what the instructor is saying and stay focused. Typically you want somewhere quiet and private, but as you get more familiarized with the techniques, you may be able to do it anywhere without anyone knowing. Some of these mindfulness techniques include mindful breathing and the body scan.

Mindful breathing sounds as it is; it focuses on your breaths without changing them. Maintaining regular breathing and listening and feeling those breaths is often used to bring people down when having panic attacks or having moments of high anxiety. It is one of the simplest forms of mindful meditation as it can be done anywhere at any time and can bring you great peace.

The body is a more visualization type of mindfulness but can be used at various points in the day, from calming your stress levels to relaxing yourself before sleep. The body scan can be done in any position but is best done either laying down or sitting.

Focusing on your body's parts, you will work your way up, acknowledging any feelings you may have in that part. Some versions of this exercise entice the visualization of the body parts in your head or a ball of light flowing from limb to limb. This exercise is put in place to allow you to individually assess how you feel in all areas of your body, indicating stress and alleviating it in the process.

Take Action

So, what are some of the things you can do to minimize your stress daily? We've looked at healthy habits, including allowing yourself the right amount of time to sleep, eating healthily, and drinking water to bring some mental clarity to your day. On top of this, try to do some simple things the night before to set up for the day. Set your clothes for the following day, packing your lunch before work days so you can grab and go in the mornings.

Taking care of your mental and physical health goes hand in hand, so when trying to alleviate stress, understanding that your body is healthy is an important stepping stone to the peace of mind you need.

Book in for your annual doctor's check-up, eye test, and skin test, and have your teeth cleaned and inspected. Making one of these appointments could change your perspective on your body and yourself and also lead to your understanding of how to help your body better. This includes brushing more regularly, drinking more water, eating specific vitamins and supplements or using the glasses.

You can try to find activities that you can perform while attending to other responsibilities, such as exercising while listening to an audiobook or podcast. You can feel confident that you will achieve your goals and satisfy your interests simultaneously if you listen to a podcast or audiobook while engaging in physical activity, such as walking, gardening, or driving to work. This will give you more time for your hobbies. Find moments to sit quietly, think, or meditate throughout the day, if you can. You should make it a point to give yourself some time to relax at least once a week, whether that's for a full day or just a portion of it and however you define it, whether it's a day without obligations, a break from intensive housework, or nothing at all. These are straightforward adjustments that can be made to lessen the effects of stress in all our lives.

One last request is to try an app or a guided meditation and try to sit and clear your mind for a few minutes. Meditation and mindfulness aren't for everyone but test them out, and it might be just what you need. It doesn't have to be incense and candles or humming music in a cross-legged position, and it can be as simple as finding a quiet place to sit and allowing yourself a moment of inner peace.

Actions steps I will complete:

Chapter 8: Checking in with Yourself

Taking the time to sit with yourself and understand where you are in life, who you want to be and where you want to go is essential. Check in with your moods, reflect on your work-life balance, and think about what is or is not serving you in your life. Think of the people you surround yourself with, the activities you get involved in, and your values and principles. Make a conscious decision to use this time to honor yourself and spend it in ways that allow you to gain insight, strength, and emotional tools for the future.

Each day is an exciting adventure and an opportunity to achieve what you have set out to do. So it's time to ask the question, who are you? If you answer by simply stating your profession, your gender, your age, or even if you are feeling overwhelmed by the question, this chapter is for you. It is about time you start figuring out who you are and making sure that person is exactly who you want to be. Life is too short to be anyone but yourself, that's for sure, but life is also too short to not even know yourself.

Journaling and Gratitude

Journaling is an excellent way to figure out where you are emotionally and can be very useful for regular check-ins. There are varying forms of journaling, whether embracing visual representations, tracking your goals, vocalizing your inner thoughts to yourself on paper, or just good old-fashioned venting. It doesn't matter what method you use to journal. However, many in the psychology field consider writing on paper to be a more personalized experience compared to using a phone or computer to type it up.

Journaling enables you to think about how you are feeling and reflect on things throughout the day that felt good or made you feel bad. This greater understanding of your emotions allows you to confront your fears, anxieties, and negative self-talk just by identifying them. If you journal regularly, which is recommended, you can track your emotions and symptoms and see a pattern in your behaviors. Maybe you can identify anxiety triggers within the words you have written on the page.

Journaling can be a stress-reducing activity that is entirely private. Even as children, we may have kept a diary with all our deepest secrets, like who we thought was cute in our class or that we stole a sibling's toy. This opportunity to be honest and express your fears and feelings will help you better understand yourself. Often we will start writing then, and all of a sudden, all our worries are laid out in front of us, contextualized in a way only we would understand.

This journal can then be used as a tool to conquer these feelings. Expressing gratitude can be a way to pull journaling from a negative perspective. Though journaling should be done in any way that brings you peace of mind and acts as an outlet for all the built-up emotions, it's essential not to allow your emotions to spiral into a dark place. Showing gratitude can be a good way not only to reflect on your day's positives but to come to an understanding of the challenges you can face during a day. Taking the time to acknowledge the small things in your day that make it better, the people in your life you cherish, or just that the weather was good are all ways to appreciate what you have.

There have been various study areas relating to gratitude's positive effects.

Though inconclusive, they are subject to providing evidence of boosting your mental health, impacting the acceptance of change, and relieving stress. Gratitude journals have become very popular and offer prompts to follow to engage your mind in thinking differently and more positively about your day and life in general. These journals offer the opportunity to reaffirm the things that make you feel good about your existence, whether it is your love for your job, seeing the friendly neighborhood postal driver, seeing a student hit a milestone, or someone cracking a joke in the teacher's lounge. What matters is being able to look at these positives expressed through gratitude and the potential stressors in your journaling and try to change your way of thinking. Changing your outlook will enable you to make and track goals, change your habits, and better understand your emotions.

Manifestations and Goals

Sometimes we can unknowingly sabotage ourselves by setting very high, very general or unachievable goals, such as "I want to be the best tennis player in the world!" This objective is unspecific. It lacks any kind of sense of direction.

A sense of direction, motivation, clear focus, and a detailed understanding of what is essential can be gained from setting goals, which are integral to every aspect of life and business. Instead of being the best tennis player in the world, maybe I want to commit to playing tennis twice every week, even if it's raining and going to get lessons to improve my serve on Saturdays at 10am.

Setting goals gives you something to work toward and a target to shoot for. Using a SMART goal as a guide can be helpful when setting goals. Specific, Measurable, Attainable, Realistic, and Timely are what the letters SMART stand for when combined to form an acronym. Because of this, a SMART goal incorporates all of these criteria to assist you in concentrating your efforts and increasing the likelihood that you will achieve your goal (Corporate Finance Institute, 2022).

Goals can be mapped out in timeframes, zones of interest (school, work, etc.), and your importance. Not all goals are going to be completed in a day, but you might have goals that you will achieve daily, such as water intake, a morning walk, a phone call to family, listening to a podcast, etc. Some goals can be life goals that you can make small sites towards.

Though setting timely goals is the last of the SMART goal guide, you can break these goals into increments that make them easier to track with an end goal being identified. Say you want to buy a home; sure, you can make a goal to buy a house, but it is not structured or specific enough and will likely fall through as it is too large of an individual goal. Try establishing a realistic financial goal toward being a homeowner, such as saving a percentage of the deposit per month based on your income surplus. Making the goals stepping stones to an ultimate goal will help boost morale as you take steps towards the bigger goal without feeling overwhelmed looking at the bigger picture.

You Time

When was the last time you were truly alone with your thoughts? There are no distractions; you can do, feel, and be however you want. This time will look different for everyone. Those with children or in the care of others will have more limited time depending on the needs of their dependents.

This doesn't mean that parents cannot have time for themselves. Sometimes it just means there might have to be a shift in how you spend this time. Suppose your time to yourself used to look like traveling far distances or going off the grid for long stints at a time. In that case, that is probably no longer possible, depending on the requirements of your family. You might have to give in to your alone time being a quick run to the store by yourself to get milk.

Maybe it's time you blast some of your favorite music instead of another rerun of the kids movie you know every word of, or maybe you want complete silence. Maybe leaving the house isn't very likely, so you just need a moment in the bathroom or an hour after the kids get put down to finally read a book you have on your list.

Laura Vanderkam, a time management expert, breaks down the time in the week and shows how to realize how much time you have outside work and sleeping—looking at the whole of your time, and finding time for yourself. In her TED talk, Vanderkam discussed her study on busy people's lives and indicated they were often likely to overestimate the amount of time they were preoccupied and underestimate the time they had to themselves.

Using the example, Vanderkam states that if you were to have an emergency that required your attention, you would be able to find time in your day to fit that in to be resolved; however, when asked to use the similar time to attend a local class as a student, do community service or spend time on yourself suddenly the time is no longer possible, because, we are simply too busy. But what if we are just lacking in prioritizing ourselves?

When was the last time you went to get a coffee by yourself? Had a long soak in a bubble bath? Read a good book? Wore a face mask? Danced to your favorite song? I don't mean a gentle sway while in the car on the way to work. I mean REALLY danced. Arms are flailing, head bobbing, letting loose kind of dance. Allow yourself to feel completely free of worries and responsibilities, and just have time to be yourself. Sure this might not sound like the right option for some people, but there are countless ways to just give yourself a break and have time with yourself. A break with your thoughts, with your dreams, with your aspirations. Just a moment to breathe in your existence without the outside noise of the world.

This time to yourself is crucial to understand what it is you want out of your life and if you feel like you are on the right track. It gives your brain a moment to breathe without thinking about anyone else but yourself. Giving yourself time to be alone can drastically improve your mental state, calming anxiety and promoting reflection on emotions. Teachers need these times of reflection and gratitude, or it may all become overwhelming. It's no easy feat educating the generations to come, and it's a consistent whirlwind of questions, responsibilities, and expectations. It's time you find time to shut that out and just listen to yourself for once.

There will constantly be varying responsibilities that keep individuals busy, whether it be work, family, hobbies, or whatever prior commitments they may have. An hour to exercise, journal, study, meditate, read and just be with yourself isn't a lot of time when you think about the number of hours in a day or even a week. There should always be time put aside for your well-being, time to reflect, heal, or be with yourself. There is always time, and it is just about making yourself a priority.

Take Action

It is time to start putting yourself first, prioritizing your happiness and wellbeing. You can do this for yourself in various ways, whether by changing habits, silencing your inner critic, or manifesting happiness while smashing goals. So step one, as it always should be, is choosing you. Choosing to commit time to yourself, taking care of yourself both physically and mentally, and making active decisions for the betterment of your life.

Try utilizing a journal to express your feelings. It can be written, typed, drawn, or collaged, and there are endless ways to do it. Ensure you are utilizing this process to allow your feelings to emerge. Your journal allows you to be true to yourself and express your emotions, fears, and anxieties. Try setting a designated time, maybe first thing in the morning or before bed. Set a timer for 5 minutes and see what your brain decides to offer you. Try to be consistent and decide if journaling helps you.

What about gratitude? You can get specifically made gratitude journals filled with prompts. Some examples of these prompts might be:

- Name something that made you smile today.
- Describe someone you love and what you love about them
- What is your favorite thing about a rainy/sunny day?
- List 5 things you like about yourself,
- Recall a happy memory, and explain why it felt like such
- Describe your favorite hobby
- What are you most proud of?

Try to use these prompts as a week of gratitude journal entries. They can be as simple or complex as you like; they are just stepping stones to change your outlook on life to see more of the positive side of everyday experiences.

Manifest your goals coming to fruition. Set one daily goal, one weekly goal, and one monthly goal. They can relate to one another or be completely different. The important part is following the SMART guidelines to ensure you understand the foundations of creating an achievable goal.

Lastly, try to find half an hour of time to be with yourself. This can overlap with your journaling or could be in addition to it. Find time to do something that brings you inner peace. Something that your body and mind craves. This will depend on each individual. Some might want a bubble bath, and others want to swim laps. Regardless of what it is, find the time and give it to yourself regardless of what it is. Consistently reiterate the importance of taking care of yourself.

Actions steps I will complete:

Chapter 9: Finding your Happiness

You are so much more than being a teacher, though it may be one of your main roles and you have traits that perfectly align with what's needed in an educator - but there is no way someone could ever call you 'just' anything!

It is easy to fall into the swing of a teaching job, the commute to and from, normal home life, and a weekend on the couch. We have all been there, but are you still there? There is a difference between happiness and settling for what your life has become. It's time to get off your couch and live life a little more.

Do you have a hobby? Have you ever wanted to try something but never found the time or effort within yourself to start? Maybe it's time to try something new. It's time to prioritize your happiness above all else.

It's time to start hanging out with friends and family you always make plans with and pull out of.

Maybe it's been a while since you sat with your parents for dinner or watched a movie with your friends. When was the last time you allowed yourself the time to read a good book, sit in a park or just stroll through your neighborhood without a destination?

There are many ways to control how you perceive things, allow yourself to feel happy in the moments you can, and try to grow past and accept the ones you are not. Happiness isn't guaranteed, but you can definitely make an effort to do the things that bring you happiness.

Attitude Towards Life

Life isn't happening to you; it's happening for you. This quote is an excellent way to recenter your focus on how you perceive life and accept the things that go on in your day-to-day lives. This way of looking at life's trials and tribulations allows you to discover your perseverance, growth, and ability to accept things you cannot change.

We all have bad days, and sometimes our students won't settle, things out of your control go wrong, and there are unforeseen interruptions in class. It happens. It's not something that is happening to you, it is just happening, and it's about how we shift these thoughts and our attitude towards days like this that makes all the difference.

Happiness starts from within; we have been told this for a long time. Happiness isn't necessarily something you just wake up feeling like they do in the movies with a giant smile across their face. Some days are more complicated than others, and some will pose more problems than solutions, but it's all about how you take on these situations, process them, and reflect on them that changes everything.

The metaphor about the glass being half full or half empty can show how we actually look at the world. Looking at the glass as half empty suggests you're an optimistic person seeing it in a positive light as what you have. Whereas if you see the glass as half empty, you see just what's missing. This would make you pessimistic. There is no point in saying you're always positive; human emotions ebb and flow naturally, but how you decide to understand and respond to situations can change a lot about your life.

Seeing a tricky circumstance as a lesson learned, instead of the world being against you can open up many opportunities. Being positive will influence your emotions; if you constantly think better things are coming, you are more open to it.

You will also see things as better compared to those who are pessimistic and might consider it a downfall. Having this line of negative thinking will also change how you accept the good things in life, probably convincing yourself it's not going to last or that you don't deserve it if it does.

So why not try looking at each day as a blessing? Consider the chances it was that you, as you are, came into existence. This can be applied to anyone regardless of religious ideals or spiritual connection. The circumstances behind our lives being what they are is incredible. Being grateful for where you are and how you got there will constantly remind you of the positives in your life, whether that be the people around you, your career, your house, your finances, or even just a half-full glass of water.

Shifting Perspective

Sometimes happiness is just a single shift of perspective, and sometimes it's easy to eye-roll people saying to look on the brighter side of life. Utilizing tools to understand better how you process your emotions and how particular situations impact you can help you build your emotional intelligence and, in turn, know why you feel the way you do.

Cognitive Behavioral Therapy (CBT) aims to help you deal with problems more positively by breaking them down into smaller parts. CBT deals with your current problems rather than focusing on issues from your past. It looks for practical ways to improve your state of mind daily (Branch & Wilson, 2021).

CBT does have some very straightforward and clear principles, though when impacted by intense emotions or situations, it can be hard to remember these principles and put them to work. CBT's reputation as an effective treatment is based on continued research, discussing the link between your perception of something to how you react to it. Though often utilized in a group or individual therapy-based setting, CBT handbooks can be found online, and the basic principles can be applied individually. However, if you feel this is something that could better change your perspective, seeking a professional is always advised for a deeper understanding of the topic. Studies have shown that CBT is more effective than medication for treating anxiety and depression.

Creative Minds Thrive

Your time is essential, that has been established, but sometimes the challenge is coming up with something to engage in the time you have to yourself. Before you turn to your smartphone for the incessant scrolling, why not try out something you have always wanted to do? Maybe instead of liking and pinning DIY projects you want to do on Pinterest, you could start doing them. Teach yourself a new language using an app.

Expressing yourself through creativity has been suggested to promote overall wellbeing and happiness with ramifications seen throughout the day of creative activity. People are more likely to undertake creative outlets and activities when in a better mood than not, resulting in arts and crafts being an example of positive mental well-being. Though this might not always be the case, as art is a powerful form of expression of emotions, you are more likely to engage in creative expression when in a good mindset than otherwise.

Maybe you are more inclined to express yourself in other ways creatively. The expression that can be felt when producing music. You might not be much of a singer. You might hide when your friends run on stage for a Karaoke session! But the thing is, singing doesn't have to be for anyone else but yourself. It's a great form of expression.

You can find ways to improve and grow your range and just experience the fun behind singing your favorite song. Are you among the many people who always wanted to or started but never finished learning an instrument? Playing instruments is good for us in multiple ways, allowing for creative output, coordination, and concentration. Playing any sort of instrument can be a relaxing adventure and could lead to a whole new hobby you didn't expect. Maybe you'll end up in a rock band!

Maybe you prefer to be a music consumer, feeling the rhythm throughout your body. Doesn't it just make you want to dance? Whether in your living room or with a dance group, you can express many emotions through dance and convey many meanings behind the music. If you think dancing is an expression you want to follow, why not see what local dance groups are in your community. Try a hip-hop class!

Crafts don't have to take a ton of time, and you don't have to be good at them. These activities are similar to hobbies for one simple reason: enjoyment. However, some people use their craft and hobbies and can turn them into a profitable side business. Sometimes creating a cash flow through creating small home-based businesses to sell at the local markets. Some people can even make a full-time career out of these activities.

Assuming you love your position as a teacher, there are many ways to utilize these things within your classroom. From finding new craft activities to do with your class in the classroom, performing short jingles on your newfound instrument, or singing a song. It's just about finding something that allows you to express yourself and participate in something that brings you true happiness.

Knowledge is Power

We are teachers, and we know the benefits learning can have on someone's self-worth, belief, and overall growth as an individual. We see it daily in the smiles of the child who just learned to tie their shoe laces and in a child moving up their reading level. Knowledge is growth. Like relearning the basics of taking care of your mental and physical welfare, learning new things will help you feel accomplished. Think about what new skills you wish to acquire.

Sure there are tertiary educational programs that can enable you to grow within your career or even let you seek a new area of expertise, such as special academic courses. These can help you grow within your career and take on more responsibility if that is what you want.

Outside educational programs, you can acquire knowledge in various areas, from reading books on topics you don't know, diving into a documentary, listening to podcasts, or watching video tutorials online. Regardless of your chosen area, it should be something that you feel will genuinely benefit you and align with your interests.

As previously mentioned, music lessons or picking up an instrument is something people often regret not doing - as it can be a skill utilized in many areas of your life but, most importantly, gives you something to work towards. Every new song or chord you learn makes you recognize the hard work you have put in for this achievement, whether big or small. This can even be utilized in your classroom, or you could offer teaching lessons as an extracurricular; there are always benefits that can work towards your professional life.

Why not try to learn a new language for your planned trip abroad or learn some ASL to be inclusive for those who struggle with their hearing. These are not only useful for those around you but for yourself. Maybe you just want to submerge yourself into a pile of books, soaking in every word and learning the history behind some of the greatest events in the world.

Sometimes learning something new can be frustrating; we can be programmed to believe that if we aren't good at something quickly, we can't do it. But persisting towards the goals will improve your mindset towards this newfound knowledge and enable you to reflect positively on your achievements.

Knowledge will always be power, whether it be a new language, a new instrument, hula hooping, dancing, or a new college degree. You feel powerful, proving to yourself and others something you set your mind to has come to fruition. You feel good when you know an answer on the local pub's trivia sheet, and you feel good with a promotion, you feel good singing and playing your music, you just feel good within yourself—That's what it has always been about in the first place.

Fun in the Sun

It's been proven that time outside can impact your physical and mental health. This doesn't mean you have to sit outside hours each day; the benefits can be seen immediately. Spending at least 120 minutes in nature per week can significantly boost your overall well-being. Regardless of the time spent, there are still many benefits.

Some benefits of being outside can be seen through physiological and psychological means. Your lungs will appreciate the break from indoor pollutants, which can be simple as just an accumulation of dust. Getting out where there is greenery will broadly impact your overall lung health, even being linked to the minimization of lung and respiratory concerns.

Similarly, being outside enables your immune system to be exposed to microorganisms that can allow your immune system to prepare a defense against a more significant strain. This is how we develop a stronger immune system. Without access and exposure to these microorganisms, our immune system would not be able to defend against viruses and diseases to the extent it can.

Enabling yourself time outside, with fresh air and sunshine, will provide your mind with clarity and can ease the symptoms brought on by the overstimulation we often experience in our daily lives.

The benefits of going outside are more than just physical. Outdoor activity can improve your mood and mental well-being, which in turn will make you less prone to depression!

Some speculate this is because the sun enables your body to produce more vitamin D or because it can be linked to getting a better night's rest, which is connected to better mental health issues. Though it could just be the simplicity and connection to the planet, hearing the sounds of the outdoors and seeing nature may present a sense of calm to those with chaotic thoughts.

Take Action

It is about time you start taking a more positive outlook on your life. We are human, and we won't always be happy at every moment, but having a positive outlook doesn't mean explicitly being happy 100% of the time but being feeling optimistic about the future.

It's time to accept the things we cannot change and work towards a life with a more positive outlook. Start to explore things that make you happy in this world from the simple yet effective time outside that enables you to feel calmer and connected to the world around you. Walk amongst the trees and sunshine and allow your body the opportunity to utilize all the good things the outdoors can offer us. Maybe it's about time you finally visit that park you live close to or time for you to tackle that hike.

Create something for fun. Make something with your hands, sing a song, and write a story. Make something that feels good to you, and express your creativity. It is about time you start up that one thing you always wanted to try, see what's available locally in classes, and get started on that long-time imagined home improvement. Take the steps needed to fill your free time with something that fulfills you.

Spend time with the people who support you. Show your appreciation for them being supportive for however long it is and return the favor. Be there for them, check in with them. Take them on an adventure and get them out of their comfort zone. Maybe there is a cooking class to attend, a mountain to climb, or perhaps you just need someone to test your crochet skills to make a scarf.

Do things that make you happy in this world, feel the sunshine even when it rains, and learn to appreciate the world around you. Run your fingers through the grass and soil and learn to process your feelings, and find what truly makes you happy.

Actions steps I will complete:

Chapter 10: Creativity in the classroom

You are more than your professional life; there is an abundance of aspects that make you who you are. All the previous chapters stated different ways to get healthy, reduce stress and give your physical and mental health the necessary attention. These steps, however, will find a way to benefit your professional life. Being an educator, the positive energy you give paying attention to your physical and mental health, will help you in your lessons, your classroom, and your relationship with your students.

It's time to continue your journey to happiness by including your life passion of being an educator. Let's look at some fun ways you can use what you've learned in the classroom.

Crunch and Sip

Healthy eating and the regular consumption of water are crucial regardless of your age. As educators, it's not only our job to take care of ourselves in this matter but promote these healthy habits to the children under our care.

Many international schools have attempted various initiatives to introduce eating fruits and vegetables in schools, from advertising the benefits of a healthy intake of fruits and vegetables.

In Australia, the Crunch&Sip initiative allowed children to snack on fruit or vegetables during a designated period between their lunch and recess. These initiatives are not only an opportunity for children to refuel during class time, whether in the middle of a lesson or as a brain break, but it also enables access to fresh fruit and vegetables. Not everyone has equal access to fruits and vegetables, and this does not exclude children. Utilizing these initiatives put in place in many international schools can help give students the chance to get natural energy from sugars and also encourage children to eat fruit or vegetables regularly.

As an educator and role model, you must show these healthy eating and drinking habits and promote them in your classroom.

Brain Break

Brain breaks are an activity put in a lesson to break up the content in some way and can have varying methods for whatever the desired outcome. Brain break activities that can both calm the students or excite them can be found online through many different resources. Students may need to calm themselves after coming in from a break in class or an activity that tends to excite the student, such as sports, announcements, or disturbances. If you want your students to focus, deep breathing brain breaks may be beneficial, as well as stretching or yoga movements, encouraging the class to stay quiet and concentrate on breathing.

Active brain breaks are used to energize and reawaken students. School can be boring regardless of the time and effort you as an educator put into fun lessons and exciting topics. Once bored, students are more likely to act up, making it hard for other students to learn. Although being disruptive is bad for a student, being unable to focus and not absorbing the information is just as problematic.

One way to re-engage students, get their focus up and reenergize the room is by using active brain breaks. These activities could be a simple 5-minute movement activity like dancing, doing stretches, playing Simon Says, and having the students copy their movements or just some basic exercises. Although there is mixed evidence from studies discussing the timeframe to settle the students back down, it helps reset the classroom atmosphere. This is just one example of allowing students to reset themselves, preventing their brains from fogging over with boredom, and keeping the energy up in the classroom. It also benefits you as the teacher, allowing you to move your body and allow the class to refocus on the activities you provided.

Tech Time

There are so many technologies out there to aid teachers in the education of students, from apps specifically for teaching to generalized apps like Youtube. Depending on your school's policy, you might be able to incorporate fun learning games into your lessons. Try using Quizlet to make quizzes based on your classes, and this can be done for all levels of students.

These quizzes allow students to work individually or collectively to come up with answers to questions written directly by you as the teacher. Therefore they can be catered to what the lessons are focused on and can be used as a warm-up to an activity or a recount of what was learned in a previous activity.

Youtube and other video-sharing apps have an abundance of child-friendly brain break exercises, stretches, yoga, songs, dances, and games. Some games teach children to spell, count, and other fun facts that can be incorporated into your lessons, such as animals, family structures, and general vocabulary. You also have access to books, documentaries, and other informative videos that your students will love and will allow you to prepare for the coming lesson.

Additionally, some apps can connect you directly to your student's parents to the goings on in the class. From their child doing a great job or potentially setting up a meeting to express concern regarding a student's progress, the communication features of these apps make a clear line between parent and teacher. These apps largely depend on the schools' agreement via policy and the parents but are helpful resources that would have been unheard of a decade ago.

Technology is great for the classroom, but it's about finding a balance between the two. There are conflicting studies relating to technology use in classrooms and the information retained when utilizing it in learning situations. Still, they provide crucial visual and auditory information that can help students who prefer learning that way. Regardless, technology is here to stay, and regardless of what is being used in the classroom, it will be used at home. So if able to, why not utilize the tools created to make things simpler for both students and you as an educator. If these tools switch up the regular flows of the classroom and allow children to learn in a different way than traditional teaching methods, it all benefits you as a teacher.

A Tidy Classroom

The simple organization is not just useful for you as an individual. It can be used in your professional life, positively impacting the students you teach and the environment you teach. It also reiterates essential life skills for the student's home life by the need to maintain cleanliness in their work and home environments.

Consider implementing a rewards program that acknowledges students putting effort into keeping the classroom clean. There are varying systems that can be put in place to track these habits. Using a sticker chart or rewards system will give students positive reinforcement for their responsibilities in the classroom. Consider offering prizes or merit awards if a student completes their task every day for a week. Maybe have an alternating chores cart, so everyone has a differing responsibility each week. It doesn't have to be a complicated process or a significant time sync, but your students will appreciate it, as will your school's janitorial staff.

These simple award programs will not only give the students positive reinforcement for keeping their space tidy but also teach them responsibility. Maybe these tasks have a designated time each day, and you can use this time to ensure your space is also clean. Sure, there will always be books, pens, things to be marked, and the regular teaching necessities on your desk, but maybe it is about maintaining a simple system. Students witnessing your willingness to clean will also reiterate the idea of keeping your space and making them feel independent in their duties.

There are multiple ways to ensure your classroom is clean, and giving the responsibility to your students and yourself is an important teaching opportunity that should be utilized. It isn't a complicated activity and doesn't have to be extensively planned, but it should be a goal within your classroom to maintain cleanliness.

Reflection and Emotional Intelligence

Asking students to check in with themselves isn't just suitable for the student but for you as the teacher. Yes, you can create this into a task, asking the student to describe their feelings, what they like about themselves, what they want to do for an activity, etc.

But you can also utilize this to ensure your students engage with the work and see what language skills they need to improve. If you ran this exercise at the beginning of the day and asked your class to write a sentence or circle a word of how they felt today, you can see who is excited, tired, happy, sad, or whatever they may answer. Activities like this can help you understand the mentality of that student and potentially work towards improving their mood throughout the day.

Not only is this a fast start to the daily task, but you can make a structure of talking about emotion regulation with them also, teaching them about emotions and how to handle them. This might be beyond your scope, but as teachers, we want to establish trust and understanding with our students. Enabling your students to learn these practices will help you process them also and reiterate the expectations of your own ability to manage your emotions.

Reflection is also an excellent way to establish goals with the students, whether it be a goal associated with a particular skill or an educational goal. These goals could be as often set as you want, whether a start of term goal or weekly; both have their place to encourage students.

Use gratitude prompts at the end of your day to start a discussion with your students about what parts of the school day they like. Avoid giving them the option to answer time on the playground and keep it focused on the lessons. Not only will this help you understand what interests the students and keep them engaged, but it will also help them recall what they learned, which is essential when trying to retain knowledge.

Some of these prompts could include:

- What were you most surprised to learn today?

- What was your favorite storybook of the day and why?
- What made you smile in class today?
- What are you excited about tomorrow?
- What is one thing you wished your teacher knew about you?

These just open up the possibilities for the students while also recalling different aspects of the day. Get involved, use this as an opportunity to reflect, and give gratitude to the class. Say moments you enjoyed, made you smile, or surprised you about your students that day.

For both children and adults, emotional intelligence is linked to many significant outcomes. Children who have higher emotional intelligence are more empathic, more able to pay attention, and more involved in their studies. They also have more positive relationships. They also control their behavior more effectively and achieve better grades. Adults with higher emotional intelligence have better relationships, more positive attitudes toward their jobs, and, for teachers, in particular, less stress and burnout at work.

If students can understand their emotions, where they come from, and why they happen, teaching will be more straightforward and less draining. Children are still finding their footing in the world, and learning things can be very stressful for their developing minds. Using the tools of reflection and breaking down emotions is the first step toward emotional intelligence, but you must be patient. These things are not always easily implemented, especially when emotions run high.

Crafty Kids

Putting creativity front and center can be particularly effective for students who find it difficult to retain information from just reading assignments and traditional lectures. In the classroom, art is essential and offers students a variety of benefits. Educators can maximize that potential by preparing to include creative practice as a focal point in the curriculum and demonstrating to decision-makers how these initiatives can have transformative effects.

According to researchers from the Johns Hopkins University School of Education, integrating creative activities into the classroom and making them a priority for academic growth increases the effectiveness of instruction.

Imagination-based learning can benefit students' social and emotional well-being by assisting them in exploring new ideas and making connections between disparate concepts.

Young learners' imaginative activities can help them develop better social and emotional regulation abilities. K–12 art classes expose students to problem-solving strategies that open their eyes to new perspectives and give them access to creative areas of knowledge. Kids may become interested in producing increasingly realistic representations and learning new techniques as they learn how art can help them express their own ideas. The development of these methods and artistic expressions continues throughout the academic years, enabling the students to express their developing perspectives.

Integrating creative arts into lessons isn't new; we use songs to teach the alphabet and coloring to learn how to add and subtract in math class. It is about making these connections through varying forms of creative expression, including music, acting, drawing, or dancing. They can act out their characters when we get our class to read aloud.

If we teach our students about particular animals, we may allow them to draw them, act them out or mimic their sounds. Create movements or dances representing your learning subjects, like new countries or cultures. These movements could even be an excellent opportunity to implement teaching ASL signing to students, allowing the action to trigger memory but also expanding their knowledge on accessibility options for those without or with affected hearing.

Using the arts as a teaching method will aid students' memory retention while giving them access to expression in a fun yet educational way. It's also a way to integrate your interests with the students, allowing you to spend some time being creative. Maybe you have always wanted to play guitar but can never find time; perhaps it is worth learning nursery rhymes and a few educational jingles. It doesn't have to be complicated, and it just has to open up the opportunity for your students to have more access to ways of learning outside the traditional reading and writing and allow you the creative challenge to make these integrations into an educational opportunity.

Actions steps I will complete:

Conclusion

As teachers, we help educate our students, supporting them throughout their day. But often, we are left with little energy to put effort into taking care of ourselves. There are many facets to self-care, happiness, and general wellbeing. It is not a one size fits all approach as we all experience and respond to things differently.

Some people out there may have a great grasp on maintaining work and self-care habits, like doing the laundry, prepping meals and tidying the house - but may lack the ability to allow themselves time to focus on things that make them happy and self-reflect on their lives. Others may be staying up too late chatting with close friends, then woke up too late and had to run out the door for work the next morning without any breakfast, to avoid being late.

Self-care is about finding a balance between what you need or want to do to lead a healthy and happy life. Our lives are not consistent, and there will always be outside factors that challenge our ability to maintain our habits and schedules. If we as educators can make adjustments in the classroom and implement strategies to overcome these disruptions, we also need to be flexible to change outside school too.

Use the technology that we have in a healthy way that allows you to grow and experience the world. Find the life that suits you, the life you picture for yourself, and utilize the strategies listed above to reach some of those goals and milestones you dream of. Find the ability to find happiness in the small things and challenge yourself to conquer the bigger things. Professionally, personally, and socially grow to the person you want to be.

Sure, drinking water and eating healthy food might not seem to tip the scale for you to be happier, but it is about how each step connects with your deeper subconscious. After all, self-care at its core is all about taking care of yourself, through tasks big or small. It's there to make you step away from the chaotic world and allow yourself time with yourself, your emotions, nutrition, your rest, your hobbies, your goals, your dreams.

Being an educator opens you up to a lot of critique, stress, and situations that can be completely overwhelming. It won't always be easy; sometimes, you might question your motivations and even think about giving up. Sometimes you need a break, but sometimes it is about pushing through and doing what needs to be done.

As an educator, you become aware of the processes of creating routines and learning new subjects, habits and skills. Finding self-love, self-satisfaction, and changing your habits and routines is not something that can happen overnight. It needs consistency and habitual effort, and sometimes there will be disruptions - this is how life works. It is about making sure you identify yourself as a priority, allowing them time to be with you and care for your physical and mental wellbeing.

Last thoughts

You can read countless books telling you how and why you should start prioritizing yourself in your life. But it begins with you deciding that you're ready to make the changes to better your life. If you can make one positive change in your life after reading this book, you have achieved a lot!

Maybe it's a new sport, a new hobby, or a quick checkup at the doctors.

But the power of these strategies really becomes more evident when you start doing these new habits consistently over the coming weeks and months. Will today be the day you start to turn your life around?

Here are a few small things you can try today:

- Set a weeknight bedtime. Set alarms and be sure you aren't drinking coffee too late in the day or make the switch to decaf.
- Drink more water. Aim to start with one big bottle a day, refill it whenever you can, and carry it with you always.
- Implement some meal prep into your life to include more nutritious snacks and meals. Try it out with fruit and vegetables to start to make healthy snack options.
- Get your body moving, even if it's just one walk around the block each morning or walk each day around the school grounds during lunchtime.
- Start essential self-care by grooming your hair, brushing your teeth, and adding a simple element of skin care daily. Wear SPF daily from now on.
- Watch your screen time and decide what apps are worth your time and what aren't. Consider uninstalling any apps you spend too much time on that don't serve a purpose.
- Find a method that reduces your stress, such as a meditation that you can do every day—allowing yourself to make habits to make life just that little bit easier to manage.
- Start a gratitude journal, acknowledge the things that make you happy in life, and make goals to do more of those things.

- Find a way to express yourself in art, dance, or drama creatively.
- Try to shift your perspective on your daily struggles and see them as an opportunity to grow.
- Be the best teacher you can be by caring for yourself as you would your students.

It's time you prioritize yourself. You find the time to make these simple changes and reach for a better life. Making progress towards finding happiness within yourself isn't about overhauling everything in your life in one swift motion. Small steps can lead to big results. It's time to change your life and finally find happiness and become the best teacher you can be - inside and outside of the classroom.

****

Thank you for reading this book! If you enjoyed it, I would be forever grateful if you could leave a review online. Your support means the world to me and an independent author. Thank you.

Enjoy the next book in this series:

References

8 Ways Being Outside Can Improve Your Health and Well-Being. (2022, May 28). Healthline. https://www.healthline.com/health/health-benefits-of-being-outdoors

American Sleep Association. (2018, December 12). Sleep Statistics - Research & Treatments | American Sleep Assoc. American Sleep Association. https://www.sleepassociation.org/about-sleep/sleep-statistics/

Branch, R., & Wilson, R. (2021, December 29). What Is Cognitive Behavioral Therapy? Dummies. https://www.dummies.com/article/body-mind-spirit/emotional-health-psychology/psychology/cognitive-behavioral-therapy/what-is-cognitive-behavioural-therapy-267176/

Brauah, N. (2021, December 25). 9 Vitamin Supplements for your Hair and Skin. Prestige Online - Thailand. https://www.prestigeonline.com/th/beauty-wellness/wellness/10-vitamin-supplements-hair-and-skin/

Chaffey, D. (2022, March 29). Global social media statistics research summary 2022. Smart Insights. https://www.smartinsights.com/social-media-marketing/social-media-strategy/new-global-social-media-research/#:~:text=58.4%25%20of%20the%20world

Cherrier, H., & Belk, R. (2015). Decluttering. The Wiley Blackwell Encyclopedia of Consumption and Consumer Studies, 1–2. https://doi.org/10.1002/9781118989463.wbeccs201

Conner, T. S., DeYoung, C. G., & Silvia, P. J. (2016). Everyday creative activity as a path to flourishing. The Journal of Positive Psychology, 13(2), 181–189. https://doi.org/10.1080/17439760.2016.1257049

Corporate Finance Institute. (2022, May 7). SMART Goal - Definition, guide, and Importance of Goal Setting. Corporate Finance Institute. https://corporatefinanceinstitute.com/resources/knowledge/other/smart-goal/

Dement, W. C., & Vaughan, C. (1999). APA PsycNet. Psycnet.apa.org. https://psycnet.apa.org/record/2000-07284-000

Dentzel, Z. (2014). How the Internet Has Changed Everyday Life. OpenMind. https://www.bbvaopenmind.com/en/articles/internet-changed-everyday-life/

Drake, C., Roehrs, T., Shambroom, J., & Roth, T. (2013). Caffeine Effects on Sleep Taken 0, 3, or 6 Hours before Going to Bed. Journal of Clinical Sleep Medicine, 09(11). https://doi.org/10.5664/jcsm.3170

Ehman, K. (2021). When making others happy is making you miserable: how to break the pattern of people pleasing and confidently live your life. Harperchristian Resources.

Ellenbogen, J. M. (2005). Cognitive benefits of sleep and their loss due to sleep deprivation. Neurology, 64(7), E25–E27. https://doi.org/10.1212/01.wnl.0000164850.6811 5.81

Eneix, N. (2021, April 29). 25 Most Popular Social Media Sites: Top Platforms, Networks, & Apps in 2021. FANNIT. https://www.fannit.com/social-media/social-media-sites/

Fishman, R. (2018, August 4). 7 Ways That Life is Happening FOR You, Not TO You - Renée Fishman. My Meadow Report. https://mymeadowreport.com/reneefishman/201 8/7-ways-that-life-is-happening-for-you-not-to-you/

Hargreaves, S. (2000). Health, happiness, and a good night's sleep. The Lancet, 355(9198), 155. https://doi.org/10.1016/s0140-6736(05)72075-4

Hood, J. (2020, February 3). The benefits and importance of a support system | Highland Springs Clinic. Highland Springs. https://highlandspringsclinic.org/the-benefits-and-importance-of-a-support-system/#:~:text=Researchers%20have%20also%20said%20that

How to Manage Stress with Mindfulness and Meditation. (2021, January 21). Mindful. https://www.mindful.org/how-to-manage-stress-with-mindfulness-and-meditation/

How to Reduce Stress Through Mindfulness | Rehabilitation Research and Training Center on Aging With Physical Disabilities. (n.d.). Agerrtc.washington.edu. https://agerrtc.washington.edu/info/factsheets/mindfulness

Jaremko, M., & Meichenbaum, D. (2013). Stress reduction and prevention. Springer-Verlag New York.

Kim, J.-H., & Lennon, S. J. (2007). Mass Media and Self-Esteem, Body Image, and Eating Disorder Tendencies. Clothing and Textiles Research Journal, 25(1), 3–23. https://doi.org/10.1177/0887302x06296873

Kolla, B. P., Mansukhani, S., & Mansukhani, M. P. (2016). Consumer sleep tracking devices: a review of mechanisms, validity and utility. Expert Review of Medical Devices, 13(5), 497–506. https://doi.org/10.1586/17434440.2016.1171708

KonMari. (n.d.). About the KonMari Method – KonMari | The Official Website of Marie Kondo. Konmari.com. https://konmari.com/about-the-konmari-method/

Levenson, J. C., Shensa, A., Sidani, J. E., Colditz, J. B., & Primack, B. A. (2016). The association between social media use and sleep disturbance among young adults. Preventive Medicine, 85, 36–41. https://doi.org/10.1016/j.ypmed.2016.01.001

Mayo Clinic. (2018). Can lifestyle changes benefit your cholesterol? Mayo Clinic. https://www.mayoclinic.org/diseases-conditions/high-blood-cholesterol/in-depth/reduce-cholesterol/art-20045935

Mayo Clinic. (2020, October 14). How much water do you need to stay healthy? Mayo Clinic. https://www.mayoclinic.org/healthy-lifestyle/nutrition-and-healthy-eating/in-depth/water/art-20044256#:~:text=The%20U.S.%20National%20Academies%20of

MentalWorks. (2014). Why are fruit and vegetable initiatives in schools effective (and why are they sometimes not)?Global F&V Newsletter. Aprifel. https://www.aprifel.com/en/global-fv-newsletter-article/why-are-fruit-and-vegetable-initiatives-in-schools-effective-and-why-are-they-sometimes-not/

Mikkelsen, K., Stojanovska, L., Polenakovic, M., Bosevski, M., & Apostolopoulos, V. (2017). Exercise and mental health. Maturitas, 106(106), 48–56. https://doi.org/10.1016/j.maturitas.2017.09.003

Mineo, L. (2018, April 17). Less stress, clearer thoughts with mindfulness meditation. Harvard Gazette; Harvard Gazette. https://news.harvard.edu/gazette/story/2018/04/less-stress-clearer-thoughts-with-mindfulness-meditation/

Nedra Glover Tawwab. (2021). The set boundaries workbook : practical exercises for understanding your needs and setting healthy limits. Tarcherperigee, An Imprint Of Penguin Random House Llc.

NSW Government. (n.d.). Crunch&Sip® - Healthy lifestyle programs for primary schools. Www.health.nsw.gov.au. https://www.health.nsw.gov.au/heal/schools/Pages/crunch-and-sip.aspx

Peters, B. (2020, May 4). The 6 Best Ways to Relax Before Going to Bed. Verywell Health. https://www.verywellhealth.com/favorite-ways-to-relax-before-bedtime-and-improve-sleep-3014977

Pontzer, H., Yamada, Y., Sagayama, H., Ainslie, P. N., Andersen, L. F., Anderson, L. J., Arab, L., Baddou, I., Bedu-Addo, K., Blaak, E. E., Blanc, S., Bonomi, A. G., Bouten, C. V. C., Bovet, P., Buchowski, M. S., Butte, N. F., Camps, S. G., Close, G. L., Cooper, J. A., & Cooper, R. (2021). Daily energy expenditure through the human life course. Science, 373(6556), 808–812. https://doi.org/10.1126/science.abe5017

Powell, A. (2018, April 9). Harvard researchers study how mindfulness may change the brain in depressed patients. Harvard Gazette. https://news.harvard.edu/gazette/story/2018/04/harvard-researchers-study-how-mindfulness-may-change-the-brain-in-depressed-patients/

Ray, R. (2021). Setting boundaries. Pan Macmillan Australia.

Ryan, K. (2016). An Overview of What Happens When We Sleep. The Journal of the YNCA Youth Neuroscience Clubs of America, 1(3), 6–7. https://youthneuro.org/media/pdf/journal/releases/0103_mNe6NOH.pdf#page=7

Summer, J. (2022, April 14). Eight Health Benefits of Sleep. Sleep Foundation. https://www.sleepfoundation.org/how-sleep-works/benefits-of-sleep

Suni, E. (2020, October 23). How Sleep Works: Understanding the Science of Sleep. Sleep Foundation. https://www.sleepfoundation.org/how-sleep-works

Taggart, L., Ozolins, L., Hardie, H., & Nyhof-Young, J. (2009). Look Good Feel Better Workshops: A "Big Lift" for Women with Cancer. Journal of Cancer Education, 24(2), 94–99. https://doi.org/10.1080/08858190802664594

University of Florida. (2020, January 28). The Importance of Art Education in the Classroom - UF Online. MA in Art Education Program Online at UF. https://arteducationmasters.arts.ufl.edu/articles/importance-of-art-education/

University of Rochester Medical Center. (2019). Journaling for Mental Health. Rochester.edu. https://www.urmc.rochester.edu/encyclopedia/content.aspx?ContentID=4552&ContentTypeID=1

Updated, S. K. P. (2018, January 15). 5 hobbies that boost happiness. Chatelaine. https://www.chatelaine.com/living/5-hobbies-that-boost-happiness/#:~:text=Crafting%2C%20knitting%2C%20baking%2C%20singing

Vanderkam, L. (2017). How to gain control of your free time [Youtube]. TEDTalks. https://www.youtube.com/watch?v=n3kNlFMXslo

Weslake, A., & Christian, B. (2015). Brain Breaks: Help or Hindrance? (pp. 38–46). https://research.avondale.edu.au/cgi/viewcontent .cgi?article=1003&context=teachcollection#:~:tex t=Brain%20breaks%20in%20the%20classroom& text=Enhanced%20learning%20through%20mov ement%20(educational,mind%20body%20syste m%20is%20activated.

Zhang, L., Adique, A., Sarkar, P., Shenai, V., Sampath, M., Lai, R., Qi, J., Wang, M., & Farage, M. A. (2020). The Impact of Routine Skin Care on the Quality of Life. Cosmetics, 7(3), 59. https://doi.org/10.3390/cosmetics7030059

Made in the USA
Las Vegas, NV
03 September 2024

94740011R00098